Passing M to the Grave

A Woman's Rise from Darkness
A Memoir by
SHERYL ARONSON, MFT

To Bunny -

Thank you so much for
supporting me and waiting
2 years for this to manifest.

Love!
Shey

KL
PUBLISHING GROUP
P.O. BOX 65053, LOS ANGELES, CA 90065
www.klpublishinggroup.com

The memoir *Passing Myself Down to the Grave* is a true story. The screenplay *Passing* was also written by the author, conceived in 2013.

KL Publishing Group
P.O. Box 65053
Los Angeles, CA 90065
www.klpublishinggroup.com

Unless otherwise indicated, Scripture quotations are from the Holy Scriptures, a gift to the author from the Rabbi mentioned inside this memoir.

Printed in the United States of America

First Printing 2018

ISBN-10: 0692131191 (klpg.)
ISBN-13: 978-0692131190 (klpg.)

This book is dedicated to my children Neil and Claire. If it weren't for God, this book would not exist. My sincere appreciation.

Contents

Acknowledgments

I am so grateful to the wonderful people who gave me so much love and support through the darkest period of my life. Without them believing in me and lending a helping hand, my fate could have been very different. The fact I am here writing these words is a miracle.

The very first person I must acknowledge is my sister, Jodi Gladstone. My sister's constant love and strength provided the stability of a safe place for me to always fall back on. The door was always open to her heart. Thank you, Sis.

Next I want to thank my two superb children, Neil and Claire Aronson. I am so proud of both of them and all their accomplishments in their young lives. They continued to thrive throughout the years when I was struggling with physical and mental health. I love both of them with all my heart. I would also like to thank my former husband, Dr. David Aronson, for being the best father to our children and taking over the parenting when I was unable.

There were three friends who stayed by my side throughout the seven years I shut out all people. Even when I could barely speak or laugh at anything, these friends always made time to see and encourage me. Dr. Lisbeth Gant-Britton, whom I have known since 1976. Thank you. I know you never stopped chanting for the "Sheryl" who walked down to the grave . . . so I could return to my former self. Even when I gave up all hope, you never did.

The same goes for Dr. Dina Martin, whom I met when our sons were in first grade. I know how much you worried sick over my mental health and prayed for my return. Thank you. Lastly, a big thanks to my friend since the 1980s, Gabriel Magyar, who sat by my side many a day when I was in pain after surgeries to talk and comfort me.

A huge heartfelt thank you to my former boyfriend of seven years, Don Wysocky, you were my rock throughout the worst period of my life and continued to protect and love me the best he could manage.

Present day, thank you to my dear friend Suze Angel, who took me under her wing when I was ready to begin socializing again in February 2013; to my writing teacher, MaryAnn Easley, and all of her writing classes, where I read excerpts from my memoir and developed my manuscript; to my dear friend and owner of *The Hollywood 360*, Linita Masters and to my fabulously creative friend, Mikey Adam Cohen who believed in my writing enough to team up with me these last few years. A final thank you to Kaylene Peoples, Founder/Editor-in-Chief of *Agenda* magazine, who made it possible for me to publish my book.

And thank you to all of my new friends!

To all cancer survivors, THANK YOU FOR FIGHTING AND OVERCOMING YOUR OBSTACLES. *Passing Myself Down to the Grave* is for you!

Credits

Book Editor, Layout, & Cover Design: Kaylene Peoples
Copy Editor: Lee L. Peoples
Cover Photo: Nathan Dumlao (@nate_dumlao)
Photo of Sheryl Aronson Journalist: Mikey Adam Cohen /
(twitter.com/Workin4Good)
Publicity: First Take PR (firsttakepr.com); Sheryl Aronson's
Headshot Courtesy of First Take PR (Photo by: Kaylene Peoples)
Publisher: KL Publishing Group (klpublishinggroup.com)

Foreword

Setting the Stage
(January, 2014)

If you suffer, if you lose your way so completely and believe there's no path back to life, this book will speak to you. If you plunge into the dark, scary places of your soul by circumstances out of your control, or if you choose to visit this place voluntarily because you think darkness is what you deserve and happiness eludes every step you take, know that I have been there, and successfully returned to the light.

Twelve years ago I was diagnosed with breast cancer. Up to this point, I had been the poster girl for health, optimism, playfulness, and adventure. I lived in the light of pursuing and attaining my dreams. My spirit throughout my life soared above the clouds of limitation, fighting off obstacles and fears in my path that tried to stop me. I tucked away any hint of pain, or sorrowful events, ignoring their icy footprints, frozen on my psyche. As I turned 48, preparing to fight the disease of cancer, these footprints melted rapidly into a pool of depression, and the portal to the grave opened. I walked inside, completely unaware of my descent into the Hades of my existence.

My journey back into LIFE occurred by passing through what I call "12 years of Despair." During this time I never believed I could burst out of the pool of hope ever again and breathe the sweet air of life's pleasures. Death beckoned, and I was ready to succumb. Down I fell, dragging a black cloak over my spirit, suffocating all character traits that were familiar to me; and I no longer recognized myself. The *Sheryl* I knew had died.

Just yesterday I found myself in a heated argument with the producer/director of the two 10-minute screenplays I had written over why he should not kill off Cleo, the 40-year-old heroine of my movie *Passing*. For artistic purposes, he had his reasons for killing her off at the end. I couldn't disagree with his logic, but something inside of me screamed, "NO! She must live so there is hope." We decided to have two endings and poll the audience to see which one they preferred. But I kept wondering why his decision to kill Cleo seemed like heresy. Not until I wrote these first paragraphs did I understand why.

For me, Cleo has to live because I lived, emerging reborn, a new woman rising from the ashes of death. I came back to my children, just like she returned to hers, wanting to live. We both took our children's hands and walked back into life with a new spirit, asking them to forgive us for any pain and anxiety we had caused.

I'm not trying to change your mind about creating two endings. But this is "my ending," which really is my beginning back into life. Writing these scripts, claiming myself as a "writer" is the first sign I'm carving my path for the rest of my life. Thank you for bringing the characters to life of Passing *and* Down to the Grave *on film . . . I'm fulfilling a lifelong dream.*

To all you Cleos, please know that there is hope. My story may be your story. My story may help you emerge from your own cocoon of despair. I didn't know why I chose the titles "Passing" and "Down to the Grave" when I wrote these movies. I just trusted my instincts. Now I know why. My spirit soars again, wiser, aware of depression's abyss. *Passing Myself Down to the Grave* is my story.

Passing Myself Down
to the Grave

CHAPTER 1
Waking Up

Passing, the Movie
(January, 2014)

EXT. FOREST - SUNRISE

The sun rises on Cleo's face as she lies on the damp ground. Iridescent light shimmers off her skin like a morning's blessing. Suddenly, the cold damp earth screams reality through her arms and legs with a penetrating icy push upwards.

CLEO sits up quickly. Her head is still fuzzy from overdosing on sleeping pills and tequila. She then looks up to the sky and realizes she is still alive.

SHE raises her right fist to the heavens.

CLEO
(Screams)
Why?

Cleo mirrors my outrage.
No matter how we try
to hide or bury the pain,
the universe will wake
us up to our fears.

Waking Up
The Memoir

Waking up. 2002. I discovered the lump on top of my right breast the year before. I felt the swelling mass time and time again with my fingers, knowing this foreign growth did not wish me well. However, the mammogram showed no signs of malignancy. I trusted my doctor. After all, wasn't he the expert?

Waking up. I stood in front of the mirrors in my bathroom, naked from the waist up, rubbing the knob. This had become a daily ritual. I hid my creeping discomfort from my children and husband. I didn't want them to know how panicked I was. According to me, I must always be in perfect health, coach softball, drive the carpool, arrange play dates, volunteer in the classroom, and make the children's lives secure and safe.

As a wife, I must work alongside my husband as a fellow psychotherapist, arrange the social calendar, be available sexually, be strong, be confident, and most of all, be a supportive partner. But with each obsessive rub of that lump above my right nipple, the role I was used to playing so well was disintegrating. For the first time in my active, all-consuming life, I woke up with an anxiety that consumed my body. No matter what techniques I used, whether psychological or spiritual, that anxiety mercilessly rushed into my system. The saying, "Physician, heal thyself," was my mantra, yet I had no access to my own bag of tricks.

Waking Up. I loved my life. I had a successful private practice with my husband in Laguna Niguel. I taught seminars on relationships and women's self-esteem. I wrote self-help articles for a local magazine. My husband and I have been expert relationship therapists on the *Montel Williams* show. A few months ago, I did a guest appearance on the *Berman Sisters* show in Los Angeles, once again addressing the audience's concerns about relationships. I've been interviewed on numerous radio shows. At this very moment, I felt my creativity exploding as never before as I became a playwright and an author of a musical on relationships called "On the Road to Your Heart." It never occurred to me that life would throw me a curve ball and stop my progress in its tracks! Nor did I ever think my own body would turn against me. When I wrote "The End" on the last page of my musical, I felt exhilarated to have achieved what seemed like an impossible dream. But little did I know my 48 years of a successful run would possibly come to an end.

Finally I faced the bitter reality. The lump I had been rubbing so diligently never disappeared. It was time to get a second opinion. Much like Satan's bold defiance of God when he said, "Take everything away from Job and see if he still believes in you." My faith in myself, and in God was about to be tested in Biblical ways. My worst fear came true.

CHAPTER 2
An Angel Is Sent

Passing, the Movie

EXT. FOREST – SUNRISE

CLEO shakes her head to clear the blurriness of her episode with tequila and pills. She turns her head forward and opens her mouth in horror. A young man about 30 stands on a ladder with a noose around his neck that he's tied around a large thick branch.

She jumps to her feet, runs over to the death stage, and scurries up the ladder.

CLEO
(Screaming)
Are you crazy? You can't kill yourself.

With trembling hands, she unties the noose.

RORY
(Screaming back)
Leave me alone. I left you alone with your tequila and pills.

Cleo ignores his remarks.

CLEO
There! Now you're free.

He looks at her disdainfully.

RORY
Not really.

Facing reality
sometimes hurts,
sometimes is scary,
but always calls for action.

Facing Reality
The Memoir

The mammogram squeezed my right breast first. A cold, sterile, yet efficient machine determined my fate. Of course I failed to stand there with any kind of dignity as I cursed under my breath. "Just relax," said the tech. I wanted to curse her too. I pretended not to mind the tech repeatedly rearranging my breast, to maximize the correct angles for the best shot.

"Now just wait for your evaluation in this room. The radiologist will be right with you."

I was sweating. I wanted to pace. I was unusually agitated.

Instinctively, I rubbed the dreaded lump, and heard my inner voice confirming what the doctor said moments later. "We need to do a biopsy right away. The tumor looks suspicious."

And I screamed inside, "Why didn't this damn lump look suspicious last year?" Now the tumor has had one full year to grow!

I was scheduled for a biopsy immediately. The feeling of panic was an unwelcomed passenger I have to drag along to an appointment. I headed toward the hospital where not only my two children were born, but also where I am on staff as a therapist. But as the patient, suddenly my workplace became my hospice. It was threatening, and in this case, ominous.

When the nurse took out the needle, I looked around for my nearest escape. Vulnerable and petrified with my breast exposed, she numbed then pricked my dreaded bump with the obscenely large needle. A sharp pain seared through my body from the pressure of the shot. This test was the first of many, which invaded my body, determining my life's outcome in the months ahead.

As I reclined on the table, isolated, I disconnected with the world. A bubble formed around me and I left my body, floated above myself, not recognizing the woman who looked so lost. I was forced to look death in the face. I stood there as a lone stranger. The protective shield of family and friends evaporated. No matter how much support and love people gave me, this new separation began to follow me everywhere. I was perpetually haunted by one thought: *"I might die. Everyone else gets to live."*

The lab technician and doctor entered the room chatting about everyday business. I want to jump off the table and shake them for being so normal, so healthy. The radiologist finally paid attention to me. "We'll call you in a few hours and tell you the results of the biopsy." I'm dismissed - Exiled to my house while I wait for the results. I waited alone in an empty house. It was the middle of the day. The last thing I wanted to do was be by myself as I'm given a possible "death sentence."

A few hours later, the phone finally rang. I stared at it numb, as it seemingly rang endlessly, breaking the deafening fog of silence that beset my kitchen. I picked up the receiver already knowing the results would not be good. The voice on the other end delivered the news, "The biopsy shows you have Stage 1 breast cancer, Mrs. Aronson. We need you to make an appointment to see a surgeon immediately."

That damn tumor . . . no longer hidden. No matter how many times I rubbed, no matter how many times I wished and prayed to God that it was a benign friend. I had to go to battle with all the weapons held in the reserves from my forty-eight years of living.

CHAPTER 3
Facing Reality

Passing, the Movie

EXT. FOREST – MORNING
Cleo looks into the tortured eyes of the young man who a moment ago
had a rope wrapped around his neck.

CLEO
(whispers to herself)
The bleak, desolate dominion of hopelessness.

RORY
What did you say?

For a moment, the morning rays of the sun frame his red hair as if
he is glowing and her heart fills up with hope for him. Like a mama
bear, she reaches up to touch his hair, but RORY whips his head to
the side.

RORY
Don't!

CLEO stares over his shoulder. Whether it was a lucid dream, or a
vision, or drug and alcohol induced . . . angels float smiling.

WHISPERINGS OF ANGEL VOICES
A choice . . . A choice . . . A choice

CLEO
(shakes her head like a dog drying off)
It's not your time.

RORY
I get to decide that.

A gunshot is heard in the distance. CLEO and RORY jump off the
ladder. RORY runs toward the sound. CLEO falls onto her knees.

25

In our darkest hour,
in our deepest despair,
the Universe (God)
sends hope.

An Angel Is Sent
The Memoir

The radiologist recommended the best surgeons for removing the cancer and I made an appointment with a doctor at South Coast Medical Center in Laguna Beach. "I don't know if I can save your nipple when I take the lump out," were the first words out of his mouth. My mind was racing. "Will my breast look distorted? well, at least I still have my breast. Why do I have to lose my nipple? Easy for him to say. He not losing his nipple. I need a second opinion."

Luckily, I followed the last thought, and my nipple to this day is still intact. The second opinion was a confident female surgeon that I knew the angels had sent me—a brilliant message is being transmitted to calm my anxiety just by hearing her name: **Dr. Police! Who else would I want to operate on me? She would track that cancer down, removing the deadly disease from my body so it would never darken my door again.**

"Sheryl, you will not lose your nipple when I do the surgery. It's not necessary," Dr. Police said with calm authority. However, just as I was high-fiving myself in my mind, she gave me news with that same authoritative voice, news I never wanted to hear. "You need to do six months of chemotherapy."

My world faded to black. Even though my husband sat by my side, I was never so alone. My worst fear came true. Going through chemotherapy was beyond terrifying, and so foreboding . . . I nearly fainted. I was a desperate salesman, knowing I couldn't change Dr. Police's mind. The doctor sat with her hands folded on the desk and patiently listened to all of my arguments and pleadings for almost 10 minutes. "Sheryl, it's the only way we can guarantee your safety, your precious health."

Who was I to argue with Dr. Police? She was now my protector. Together we would be Amazon Warriors, blazing across the battlefield of my cancer, guaranteeing victory. My fate was sealed. The virulent chemo cocktail, an incorrigible host, would ransack my body and soul even worse than the cancer itself. Knowing that this treatment of chemical poison would devastate my life, I was powerless to refuse it. My worst fears never came close to the horrors of this liquid torture that invaded into my bloodstream.

And eventually, my thick curly hair lay in clumps. I looked down from my barber chair at the back of a local wig store. Shaving my head was the panacea to an inevitable problem we cancer victims face; patches from our scalps, reminding us we are diseased like fallen branches from an infirm tree.

The cold air swept over the moonscape that is now my baldhead exposed, naked, as I painstakingly examined the hairpieces that were destined to decorate my face. A long, straight-haired wig, light brown in color called to me, as did its sister, a shorter one, same color and style. I also selected colorful, cheerful scarves as cover-ups. With my two new hairstyles bobbing in the boxes, I exited the wig shop, not recognizing my former self. The familiar had slipped away. All was lost.

CHAPTER 4
A Poet's Prediction

Passing, the Movie

EXT. FOREST – MIDMORNING

Cleo feels dizzy and unbalanced. As she tries to stand from the kneeling position, her bare feet crush the grass. Then her knees buckle, and CLEO crashes to the earth again. The sudden jolt forces her eyes open.

EXT. RIVER – MIDMORNING

An adolescent boy stands in the river placing rocks in his pockets. Then from the back of his pants, he pulls out a gun, sticks it in his mouth trying out the fit, shakes his head, no, then he pushes the gun back into the back of his pants. He then takes out a piece of paper and pencil, writes a few lines, crosses them out, and writes some more.

EXT. FOREST – MIDMORNING

CLEO
(Cries out)
That's his suicide note.

Gathering the skirt up from under her, she springs into action. Suddenly all her instincts kick in, and she knows exactly where to run.

EXT. RIVER – MIDMORNING

CLEO runs to the river's edge.

She sees RORY rush in the water toward LEVY. LEVY quickly turns around, pulls gun out and points it at RORY.

RORY
Calm down, kid. You don't want to do anything rash.

LEVY
You mean like hang myself from a tree?
Passed you by on my way here. You looked real comfortable.

RORY
Get out of the water. Let me help you.

RORY reaches for the hand holding the gun.

LEVY
Don't want your help.
If you don't back off, I'll kill you.

LEVY fires a bullet past RORY'S shoulder and collapses in the water.

RORY scurries over, grabs the gun, helps LEVY up and leads him out of the water.

CLEO
(runs into the water and helps both out.)

CLEO
You're both crazy. Guns! Nooses!

She examines their bodies for injuries and finds the rocks in LEVY'S pockets.

CLEO
Drowning. Nice touch, just in case the gun didn't blow your face off.

LEVY
See you like the soft touch. Pills... booze... death.

RORY
He passed us on the way to his execution.

CLEO sticks out her hand toward LEVY.

CLEO
Give me the note.

LEVY looks at her, surprised.

LEVY
It's a poem. Private.

CLEO
And a poem is to be passed down so the audience can appreciate the words.

LEVY
My words do not count.

CLEO
Let us be the judge.

Inspiration
transpires out of our pain.
Sometimes the heavens open up,
dropping messages in our lap.
Like Cleo, I too was given
foresight.

A Poet's Prediction
The Memoir

At the exact same time I was diagnosed with breast cancer, my cousin Robert received a diagnosis which proved to be fatal: liver cancer. Bob and I were like brother and sister growing up and had lived catty-corner to each other in the same four-family garden apartment complex in North White Plains, NY. Bob lived in Paris when he received word of his cancer. We spoke on the phone frequently during this time. He knew his prognosis was not good, but he believed he'd cure himself through holistic means; he contacted the Gersten Clinic in Tijuana, Mexico, and was admitted there for treatment.

Bob was now only two hours away in Tijuana, instead of 11 hours away in Paris. I visited him as often as possible; but each time I went there with my sister, he seemed to slip farther away. His legs were swollen from the carrot juice detox and strict vegan diet. I hated seeing him so withdrawn . . . and a little confused.

But he fought daily for his life and stayed convinced that this holistic approach would work.

We had many conversations about what happens after we die, and we both believed our spirit goes on even if it is not connected our physical body. One day I asked Bob, "How are you going to contact me after you pass?" He answered simply, "We both grew up in a place called Edgebrook, so I will contact you through that name or the meaning of that name."

Bob moved to hospice care in San Diego after being at the Gersten Clinic for a few months. The last time I saw him, the Angel of Death lurked inside. His eyes were wide open like black, vacant coals. He sat in the wheelchair hunched over as if all the life had been sucked out of him. "This is not my Bob!" I screamed to myself. "This is not my Bob who taught me about literature, writing a perfect sentence. This is not the young man I had a crush on as a young girl, and to whom all the boys I ever went out with after that needed to measure up. This is not my Bob who speaks French fluently, living life to the fullest as a bohemian artist in Paris with his lovely wife, Joelle." Then my ranting stopped.

Bob will be returning to his whole self when he passes. Only he knows what will happen, and I blessed his leaving.

I knew the moment Bob passed. It occurred on a humid summer's day when I was taking my daily walk along a canyon pass. As I was walking down the street heading toward the path I usually take, two unusual occurrences happened. I heard the bubbling sound of water happily calling out to me. Even though I had taken this walk many times before, I had never heard the sound of water. Immediately I thought of Edgebrook, the housing development where we both grew up. (It was called that because it was next to a babbling brook.) "Bob," I cried out. "You're telling me it's your time . . ." The next moment two ravens cawed loudly in a tree high above me. They wouldn't stop, or maybe they were releasing the death cry. It's as if they wanted me to stop and pay attention to the moment to honor the sacred seal of death. I had a conversation with two ravens. "I'm listening. What are you telling me? Is Bob gone?" I continued my walk and silently relived memories of my beautiful, sensitive cousin.

After my walk, I returned to the spot where the ravens spoke to me. Strangely, they were still there. Again, they let out unrelenting loud caws. I just knew this was the end of Bob's journey here on earth.

When I got home, I phoned his wife Joelle. She told me that she had just returned to Paris from San Diego after going to the Gersten Clinic and transferring Bob to a hospice facility. Because the Clinic saw that they could no longer help him, it was imperative he be put elsewhere for his final days. Joelle continued to say that she had stayed with him for over a week, but had to return to Europe because of her teaching commitments.

That's when I told her about the ravens. She was silent.

"Sheryl, I looked out my window just the other day, and I saw something I hadn't seen in the 10 years I'd lived in my apartment. A whole flock of blackbirds flew by, darkening the sky." My heart filled with awe at the mysterious connection of our two stories. Joelle continued. "And I knew . . . Bob's end was near."

We were silent for a moment and allowed the sacredness of this occasion to sink in. Six thousand miles apart from each other, we were feeling the love from Bob's spirit. He died the next day. A few days later, feathers appeared on the ground for no apparent reason. I looked down on the sidewalk and there was a feather. At first I thought coincidence? But more feathers kept materializing. I had no doubt that Bob was communicating with me from the other side. His brother Howard had Bob cremated in San Diego. Joelle arranged a memorial service in Paris a few weeks later. My sister and I attended. Joelle asked people to speak at the memorial and I volunteered.

About 30 of Bob's friends in Paris were gathered in Joelle and Bob's flat in a suburb of Paris, Maison Alfort, to share stories about this brilliant man. I told my story about the ravens in English since I didn't know French. At the end of the memorial service, I was approached by a woman who told me a story about her experience regarding Bob's death.

"Bob was one of my very dear friends. I hadn't been in touch with him since he went to Mexico and stayed at the Gersten Clinic for his treatment. I was taking a holiday in Morocco at the beach. One day Bob's face popped into my mind and I didn't know why. Then I noticed two feathers were crisscrossed on the ground, and I felt his presence so strongly at this point, but had no idea what all this meant. Now I know." My heart filled with joy as she relayed her story. I called Joelle over, and all three of us basked in the blessings of the birds and feathers.

And feathers continued to show up throughout my "12 Years of Despair," offering me a sliver of hope in the darkest hours. Even when it was impossible to smile or laugh, seeing a feather made me smile inside. The story about Bob took place after I experienced chemotherapy in the spring of 2003. The raven (the black bird) was an omen, predicting his death. My bird's color is white. And she came to me in a dream right before I began my cancer treatment in the summer of 2002.

CHAPTER 5
The White Bird

Passing, the Movie

Cleo, Levy, and Rory sit by a campfire warming their wet bodies.

CLEO looks at her children's picture in one hand, kisses pictures, places it on the ground. As if in a trance, she picks up the gun LEVY has by his side. She is fascinated by the hard, sleek feel of it in her palms. She turns it over in her hands again and again.

CLEO
Violent. Harsh. Quick. Decisive.

FADE TO:
INT. OFFICE - DAY

LEVY sneaks into his mother's desk and takes out a gun. He points it at his head, puts it in his mouth, weighs it in hand, points it at his chest, half pulls the trigger, then reverently places it in the waist of his pants. His left eye is swollen and tinges of black and blue paint on his eyelid. He leaves a note where the gun was. Shuts the desk drawer.

FADE TO: INT. BEDROOM – DAY

CLEO examines her breasts in the mirror. She takes each one in her hand, like she's never seen them before. Above the left breast is a nasty red scar that looks like a small zipper and underneath the skin she still feels the catheter that acts as the portal for the chemo. She keeps rubbing her hands over the scar as if still in pain. The rubbing becomes more persistent. Beside her is a bottle of tequila from which she drinks, then pops a pill. The scarlet scar stands out like it's mocking her. She rubs it over and over again.

FADE TO: EXT. IN FRONT OF A GIRL'S DOORSTEP - NIGHT

RORY picks up an engagement ring from the ground. He turns it over and over in his hand. He looks at the dark window. Everything around him looks bleak, barren. He takes off his belt and ties a noose with it. Slips it over his throat.
A light goes on for a second.
He looks up with hope.
But, then it shuts off again.
He pulls the belt tighter around his throat.

CUT TO: EXT. TREE - MOMENTS LATER

Both guys hover over CLEO as she spins the gun faster and faster in her hands. She is mumbling to herself now.

CLEO
I'm no one's future. I'm no one's future.

LEVY bends down to her at eye level.

LEVY
Don't say that. It's not true.

LEVY
(She puts her children's pictures back in her hands.)

This is your future. Don't take it away from your kids . . .

LEVY takes the gun away from her.

CLEO
What do you two know about life? Suffering? You're just starting out.

CLEO grabs the gun again from LEVY and points it at her face.

LEVY and RORY lunge toward her and grapple for the gun.

As everyone struggles, the gun goes off, a bullet hits LEVY in the shoulder.

CLEO and RORY look horrified.

LEVY is calm. He wipes his hand over his blood.

LEVY
Blood. My blood.
I didn't think I had the guts to shoot myself but you did it for me.

(He walks over to CLEO who has the gun in her hand and gently takes it away from her.)

LEVY
This is how it feels. AAHHHHHH!!!

CLEO rips off her shirt and tears the sleeve to make a tourniquet for his shoulder.

CLEO
Sorry, I didn't mean to . . .

LEVY is weakening and falls into CLEO'S arms.

LEVY
The asshole said I didn't have the guts to kill myself, too sensitive.

CLEO puts her arms around him, talking softly now.

CLEO
Doesn't matter. Sit. Rest.

She lowers LEVY to the ground.
No one is going to hurt you now.

LEVY
Too late. I'm bleeding. You're lousy with a gun.

RORY
Just a flesh wound. You'll survive.

LEVY
Yup. Will survive.

LEVY faints.

A sign of hope
appears in dreams,
appears in waking life.
My interpretation
makes it meaningful . . .
or not.

The White Bird
The Memoir

The family planned a summer vacation before I had surgery to remove the tumor and begin the chemo treatments in September. I felt relieved that my focus could be on my children, husband, and fun. Before we headed to Cape Cod, we stayed in a hotel in Lexington, Massachusetts, and visited with my sister-in-law, brother-in-law, nephews, and my in-laws. I felt separated from the others because the "I am sick and you're not" mantra took over. Staying in the present was nearly impossible.

I had a dream that night which offered me some peace.

I am twisting and turning in my bed with worry about the upcoming chemotherapy treatment. My chest hurts. I can't breathe. Any second, I will explode with anxiety. Suddenly a white bird appears in the room and enters my head. It sits inside of my brain and half of its body is inside of me, while its stomach and neck stick out. Like ice melting gently, the bird's spirit of peace and love fills me. My entire being is now padded with blessings and acceptance. I know I will be okay.

When I woke up the next morning, I immediately remembered the dream. It was like a soft hand stroking me, reassuring me. I was finally able to join the others in conversation and activities without feeling isolated. The dream served as a talisman throughout my trip, but its influence was fleeting. As soon as the vacation ended, the reality of the surgery and the chemo threatened mutiny on my state of mind.

They scheduled my surgery to remove the lump, to put the catheter in my chest for the chemo infusion, and to remove lymph nodes under my right armpit in order to monitor the spreading of cancer cells. Anxiety thrashed about throughout my system, while I beckoned all my psychological and spiritual resources to keep me calm. I succumbed and finally needed to go to a psychiatrist for anti-anxiety drugs.

The night before the surgery, I couldn't sleep. Facing my mortality terrified me. Will the cancer spread? I knew I was very lucky that my tumor was only Stage 1, but that didn't mean the cancer cells hadn't attacked the other parts of my body. I went downstairs to meditate in the office where the computer and books were. A book called out to me, so I took it off the shelf. The title was *You Can Heal Your Life* by Louise Hay, a top New Age author. Without thinking, I randomly opened the book to a page and gasped in shock . . . yet my heart filled with joy. On the page was a white bird flying out of a cage. I read the explanation:

In the infinity of life where I am, all is perfect, whole, and complete. The past has no power over me because I am willing to learn and to change. I see the past as necessary to take me to where I am today. I am willing to start where I am right now, to clean the rooms of my mental house. I know it does not matter where I start, so I now begin with the smallest and the easiest rooms; and in that way, I will see results quickly. I am thrilled to be in the middle of this adventure,

41

for I know I will never go through this particular experience again. I am willing to set myself free. All is well in the world.

The magic of the moment removed my bad thoughts. My opening to that page acted as validation from the universe that the angels were watching over me. And then another miracle or unexpected event happened only a few days later. As I drove on Alicia Parkway in Laguna Niguel, a white crane flew over the Regional Park. I was no longer alone. My white bird would appear again and again throughout the next 12 years.

CHAPTER 6
Being Cut Open

Passing, the Movie

EXT. RIVERBANK - LATER IN THE AFTERNOON

LEVY lies on the ground, still out cold.

CLEO dabs her torn wet shirt on his face.

RORY holds the gun in one hand, the noose in the other.

CLEO
Choose your poison.

RORY
I've made my choice.

CLEO looks at him with a frown.

CLEO
Over my dead body . . . no way I'm letting you kill yourself.

RORY
Listen lady...

CLEO
Cleo.

RORY
Rory.

(They both nod in acknowledgement of the other.)

No one gives a shit if I die. I've burned all my bridges.

CLEO
Burned all you bridges? At 30?

RORY
Torched! Nuked! Every bridge...
Didn't interfere with your decision. Let you sleep into oblivion.

CLEO
I woke up. I always do.

RORY
You've done this before?

CLEO
Third time isn't a charm. Each time I take more pills, drink more tequila. You think killing yourself would be easier.

RORY
What's with you?

CLEO
Cancer.

She looks down at her breasts.

I kept them both but the chemo ate away more than the cancer.

RORY
You're a survivor. Isn't that the term?

CLEO
Parts of me didn't survive.

RORY
Exactly.

CLEO
What parts of you didn't make it?

RORY
All of me. None of me. Lost everything. Excuse me.

(RORY puts the gun by CLEO'S feet.)

You're in charge. This one is more final.
He walks away.

CLEO
No! RORY come back.

She places LEVY'S head on the ground, looks lovingly down at him. Stands, looks again at LEVY. Looks out to where RORY walked away. A beat. She runs after RORY.

My flesh wounds open a Pandora's Box that couldn't be closed.

Being Cut Open
The Memoir

The day of my surgery arrived. Three different parts of my body were cut: my breast, my chest, and under my right arm. In two places I lost parts of me: a tumor which invaded my body, and a few lymph nodes which determined if the cancer spread. In one place I gained something . . . a catheter, which administered the chemo into my body.

Under the light of the operating room, I stared at the ceiling, heard the anesthesiologist's voice as the mask was being placed over my face. My fate was now in the surgeon's hands. Slumber. Peace.

Bright, harsh lights of the recovery room assaulted my eyes first, like a bad hangover. Awakening, I was disconcerted. The anesthesia's numbing effects were still protecting my body from pain, so I was disoriented. Back in my room, I received the good news: the cancer did not spread into the lymph nodes, and the lump containing the cancer was removed without any loss of my nipple (just as Dr. Police promised).

And then I felt the invasion of a foreign substance, six inches above my left breast, itching, sticking out slightly through my skin, like a malevolent creature from another planet, it threatened my wellbeing . . . friend or foe?

As Dr. Police later checked on me, she promised me the catheter was a friend. "It's a much better way to receive the chemo. Your veins would harden in your arms if the chemo were to be placed there. This way you're hooked into the chemo from a drip through the catheter, and it immediately enters your body without any intrusion or damage to your veins." Her smile and confidence inspired me to believe her; however, this raw patch of skin and awkward lump mischievously looking up at me; and now . . . I had something new to rub and worry about.

Now all three parts of my body were screaming in pain. I'd been cut open in three places, and each one protested with a searing sensation. They took turns torturing my skin relentlessly. This experience was the first to chip away at my protective wall – behind a wall whose inhabitants lived in darkness . . . carefully placed there by me. All my psychic pain from the past and maybe all the psychic pain of my past lives as well. (I believe we have lived before, many times.)

Pain pills dulled the agony a little, but I discovered the sensitivity that had existed beneath my happy and tough exterior. I was an athlete my entire life. I played through the pain. And when I was hurting, I was trained not to allow that pain to hold me back, impeding my performance. If the ball hit me in the face, I stopped a moment, recovered, then put my mitt on and went back to my position. On the basketball court, if I twisted my ankle, I headed to the sidelines, walked some, shook it out if I was able to continue walking, and went back in and resumed playing. I wrapped my ankle when I got home; put an ice pack on my face where I was hit by the ball. That's it!

I had been handling myself similarly with this new psychic pain.

When someone hurts my feelings, rejects me, criticizes me, I don't show vulnerability. I keep going forward on the playing field of life. Smile. Stay positive. Make excuses for the bad behavior of others. I work harder to be a better person, take the criticisms people give me, then used their criticisms as feedback for making changes. Even now, when anxiety arises inside of me, I continue to push it back down and keep going until my nervousness disappears . . . and I always take action. I go after what I want, no matter how many times the universe puts up obstacles. No feeling sorry for myself. Move forward.

But when I rested on the couch in the family room, hurting, I asked myself, "Where are the baseball fields, the courts? There wasn't anybody around to criticize or to reject me. I was up against myself, my disease, or rather 'dis -ease'. "What do I do with myself now?" I can no longer ignore the pain. I can't ignore the tears welling up in my eyes. I can't ignore the vulnerability of my situation. "Can I build a bridge that connects my inner dark village with the present day psyche of *Sheryl*?" I had no idea the depths of my darkness. I had no idea how far I would sink into the hole of despair. The heavy lid of the grave was creaking open.

CHAPTER 7
Passing Through the Gate

Passing, the Movie

LEVY opens his eyes.

FADE TO:
EXT. RIVERBANK - MOMENTS LATER

LEVY is standing in the water. He takes out a piece of paper from his pocket.

LEVY
Does anyone want to hear a poem?

(He asks to no one. He reads.)

The river flows over my feet.
Ancient waters pass no knowledge through my soul.
I am empty to the bottom,
Like a dry vessel,
Cracked and broken.
Only a gun speaks my truth,
salvation through bullets.
A boy's body now at peace
On his way to somewhere else,
passing through existence no more.

I too am tested.

Passing Through the Gate
The Memoir

Chemotherapy. Even today whenever I see a woman wearing a scarf on her baldhead and unprotected neck, holding up a brave face, my heart breaks. I feel such compassion and sorrow all at once. I feel the heaviness of my hair now hanging all over my neck, my head, and give thanks I survived. I know her pain. I know her challenges.

Chemotherapy. Even today my body shudders whenever I see a movie and the character goes through chemo in the story. I get sick to my stomach. I feel the scar above my left breast on my chest and twist and turn my body as if trying to escape the infusion the character is experiencing.

Chemotherapy. Even today when I watch the actress who plays Cleo in the movie *Passing* receive a fake scar drawn on her chest, tears well up in my eyes. The smear of redness, the tiny gashes of surgery filled in by the makeup artist, glare at me. Once again, the raw, exposed wound seems alive. I leave the room, go to the bathroom, and cry. My sorrow runs deep. Yet I honor the battle I fought every three weeks from September 2002 to January 2003. My tears heal my release of all the pent up emotion. Now these friends reside in a safe place for expression.

Not the case January 2003. After the last round of chemo, my entire being...

> *empty to the bottom,*
> *like a dry vessel,*
> *cracked and broken.*

Chemotherapy. It was my first time. My husband drove me to the oncologist's office where the drug cocktail was to be administered. As we pulled into the parking lot, I panicked. What would the chemo feel like as it flows through my veins? Will I be able to withstand the treatment? What would happen when I get home? Will I sleep? Will I go on with my life as if nothing happened? When will my hair fall out?

None of these questions was answered until I actually experienced the medicine, the life-saving medicine that systematically stripped away every psychological defense I ever created. In some ways, receiving chemo was like having a baby. People can tell you about the adventure, but not until those labor pains thrash through your womb do you totally understand the vicious, ecstatic pain. Chemo is just vicious.

And No amount of smiling, optimistic philosophy, or spiritual centeredness could prepare me for the brutal attack on my body.

Here's what I want to say to every woman or man who has gone through this nasty business.

CRY. LAMENT. KNOW THIS. YOUR MIND, YOUR BODY, YOUR SOUL, ARE BEING TORTURED. DON'T LET ANYONE - THE MEDICAL COMMUNITY, YOUR LOVED ONES, EVEN FELLOW CHEMO PATIENTS - TELL YOU THAT THESE FEELINGS AREN'T PRODUCTIVE. IF THIS IS WHAT YOU ARE FEELING, THEN HONOR THEM. DON'T DENY THE PAIN AND THE DARKNESS THAT MIGHT DESCEND UPON YOU. BUT REMEMBER . . . WHERE THERE IS DARKNESS, LIGHT AWAITS US AT THE OTHER END. DENYING THESE FEELINGS ONLY PROLONGS THE SUFFERING . . . ACCEPTING AND HONORING THEM PROVIDES RELIEF.

No one can walk in your shoes. No one knows how fast or how slowly you process devastating occurrences. Some people receive chemo and have very little reaction to it. If so, then they are incredibly fortunate. Blessed. But we are blessed, too, we who suffer. Constructing the courage of a lion, a warrior, looms in the future. This courage is based on facing the pain, the loss, the sadness, the anger, and most frightening, death. I faced death three times. Three times after I survive breast cancer, I tried to kill myself. (I don't recommend this.) This was my path, which has taken me 12 years to complete. I'm telling you my story because I want you to have hope and know that you are not alone. I want you to know that God (or whatever you believe, the spirit of life) never abandons us. Time and time again, signs from the universe have fallen into my lap, and sometimes I recognize and use them, and sometimes they've pass over my head because I am too deeply wrapped up in my own anxiety, depression, and confusion. We all receive signs. Hardly any of us pays attention. Time to pay attention.

The oncologist's waiting room served as a holding tank before heading to the back and getting hooked up to the chemical mixture. The colors of the walls were soft, pale, subdued, nothing to cause any anxiety. Dr. Teteff comes out, shakes my hand and leads my husband and me back to the special rooms where I would be for the next few hours. I had the choice be alone in a private room, or sit with other patients. I chose to be alone. My white blood count was taken because the chemo could compromise the number, and would be dangerous if the count went too low.

I rested on a beige, leather, Easy-Boy Recliner in front of the television. To the right, hung the bags of the chemo drip. Within a few minutes, the nurse punctured the rubber piece that remained underneath my skin that opened up to a vein in my chest; and the liquid mixture was poured through my body on its mission to kill any cancer cells that lingered inside of me. I had a book and settled in.

A cool sensation of the chemo potion rippled through me. For a few hours I sat, filling up with poison. The actual experience seemed incredibly benign. What happened a few hours later, once I returned home and congratulated myself for surviving the first treatment, shattered my world.

The floodgates of destruction raged through me, and I lost control of every ounce of sanity. A relentless war forged inside my organs, bowels, and stomach, turning me inside out with no break. I puked. I puked. I puked some more. When I thought there was no more to let go of, I puked again. I sat on the toilet, releasing bowels that needed to escape. I hallucinated. I cried. I screamed for mercy, but no relief.

Hours passed. My bathroom transformed into Dante's Inferno as I twisted and turned in the hell that became my bodily functions. At some point, I fell asleep.

After two days of agony and no eating, I functioned again. Back to being a therapist, back to being a wife and a mother. But little did I know I had just taken the first steps toward the demolition of my soul.

CHAPTER 8
Descending Into Darkness

Passing, the Movie

CUT TO:
EXT. FOREST WITH BARE TREE – NOOSE HANGING -
MOMENTS LATER

RORY *rushes to the tree. He climbs the ladder and ties the noose onto a branch. Slips noose around his neck.*

CUT TO:
EXT. OPENING IN FOREST

CLEO *runs in. She slips on a rock and falls to her knees.*

CLEO
RORY!!!!! NO!!!!!

CUT TO:
EXT. RIVER

LEVY *looks up at the sky then down at his feet. He kisses the paper the poem is written on and waves it in the air. He takes the gun and places it in his mouth.*

CUT TO:
EXT. OPENING IN FOREST

CLEO *kneels on the ground, her head hanging.*

CUT TO: EXT. THE SKY.
Two white birds fly together.

My descent took place gradually.
Circumstances wore away the thin
shell of protection around me.

Descending Into Darkness
The Memoir

Normal. How could I continue to keep everything normal? My children were eleven and nine, fifth grade and third grade. I was a volunteer classroom mom, I coached my daughter's softball team, and both children attended Sunday school and Hebrew lessons. They also needed to have a social life so I planned play dates. There were endless school functions to attend, lunches to prepare, and homework to get done. Both were into acting and were auditioning for commercials, plays, and movies. Each child had landed national commercials, so this promoted further interest in obtaining more roles. My son took acting lessons at South Coast Repertory and had a role in their famous version of Charles Dickens' *A Christmas Carol* as the young Charles Dickens. More driving, more schlepping, more activity than my body could handle. But I never wavered. My first and foremost thought was, "The children need to experience normalcy. Their lives must go on as before."

Normal. I saw clients. I maintained my private practice. I refused to let the chemo take away my productivity, my energy, my positivity, my life. However, like a balloon slowly leaking air, my dynamic, vibrant, vitality was dissipating. I noticed how my body felt sluggish, like it was filling up with dirt and mud, weighing me down. At the same time my physical body was weakening because I couldn't eat. Food nauseated me. I had just lost 20 pounds, finally losing that stubborn weight I gained after giving birth to my daughter. And now without any dieting, the weight flew off my body. My hair felt like dying branches, desperate, pleading for me to let them fall to the ground. I clung to the hope that I didn't need to shave my head. Yet as the days passed, I could not tolerate the heaviness of my locks begging me to let them go. It was time to shave my head.

Normal. My body entered into premenopausal symptoms. Hot flashes struck without warning, flooding me with perspiration. With each deluge, I felt dizzy, embarrassed, overwhelmed. My physical self no longer belonged to me. My head sweated underneath my wig, and I always felt hot. Sleep eluded me, whereas before, I went to bed at 11:30 p.m. and woke up at 6 a.m. My new sleeping pattern was up at 1, 2, 3 a.m., unable to feel safe and secure in the bed, sleeping next to my husband. I needed space to experience this unfamiliar territory. In the morning, I started over. I was MOM. I was WIFE. I was THERAPIST.

Normal. The anxiety, that began its invasion on my psyche before I knew I had cancer plagued my every waking moment and probably dreamtime, too. And daily, another foreign emotion knocked on my door. Depression. I'd be damned if I let either of these toxic emotions drag me down. I continued to smile and have a positive attitude. I continued to work and be encouraging to my clients, and I continued planning social activities for the family. I continued to fight inwardly for my own normalcy.

Normal. Then there were the days after the chemo treatment where I lay on the couch in the Family Room, listless, limp, lifeless. I was a shell. I was lost in misery. Sometimes a woman from Temple Beth El came over and cooked dinner for the children. What a blessing to have this support. All I knew was I wanted to be in the center, the heart of my family, even though I was on the couch, barely functioning. The vibrant life of my family existed and I needed to drink in their activity, their breathing, my children's happiness. My husband commented to me, "Why don't you go upstairs and be by yourself?" He blew by me on his way to the office. He was frantically struggling to be the provider, take care of business, try not to show his desperation and fear that maybe his wife might die. But I didn't want to be alone. I didn't want to hide away in the empty, silent bedroom. My spirit, slowly expiring, craved the comfort of my children, my babies to whom I gave life. I need LIFE back.

Normal. Dr. Teteff recommended anti-depressants and anti-anxiety medication. My husband agreed. My fight internally was this: I HAVE NEVER BEEN DEPRESSED IN MY LIFE AND I REFUSE TO BE DEPRESSED NOW. I HAVE NEVER BEEN ANXIOUS BEFORE, AND I REFUSE TO BE ANXIOUS NOW. I AM STRONG. I AM COMPETENT. LIFE HAS BEEN GOLDEN AND I'LL BE DAMNED IF I ALLOW THIS CANCER TO BRING DARKNESS INTO MY SOUL.

Off in the corner of the Universe, GOD and SATAN meet.

Ext. PARK BENCH – DAY TIME

GOD
So SATAN, do you see my servant, my blessed subject, SHERYL? She suffers, but she never stops believing in me, in hope, in life.

SATAN
Take everything away from her and then we'll see.

60

GOD
You see how she suffers. She has cancer. Her body is being ruined by the chemo.

SATAN
Her Life is still golden.
TAKE EVERYTHING AWAY FROM HER AND SEE HOW SHE BELIEVES IN YOU, YOUR GOODNESS, YOUR LIGHT. SEE IF SHE STILL CELEBRATES LIFE.

GOD
And so I will.

I look at the doctor and my husband. I agree to take medication and go see a psychiatrist. I give in.

CHAPTER 9
Deconstruction I

Passing, the Movie

FADE TO:

INT. BEDROOM –DAY TIME – ONE YEAR BEFORE

CLEO *wakes up screaming in her bed. Her husband, DANIEL wakes up startled. He grabs her and envelopes CLEO in his arms.*

DANIEL
What happened? Are you all right?

CLEO
I was wrapped in white gauze like a mummy. The doctors said I had to wear this in order for them to operate. Then needles poked me. I couldn't breathe. My whole body filled with pain. I yelled, "Stop! Stop!" No one listened to me.

(CLEO pulls away from DANIEL. Begins to get out of bed.)

DANIEL
CLEO come back. Where are you going?

CLEO *walks over to the mirrors that lead to the walk-in closet. These mirrors reflect the mirrors on the opposite wall, which hang over the bathroom sinks. CLEO's image reflects into infinity. She lowers the nightgown so her breasts are exposed. CLEO takes her left hand and rubs the nodule that sits on top of her right breast. She stands there as if in a trance. DANIEL walks over to her and puts his arms around her shoulders.*

DANIEL
Honey, what's wrong? What are you doing?

CLEO
The lump. The damned lump. It won't go away.

DANIEL frowns. He looks closely at her breast

DANIEL
*I thought the doctors told you not to worry about it. The lump is
benign.*

CLEO pushes him away. She feels the lump again.

CLEO
The dream indicates otherwise.

DANIEL
Come on. Don't worry. You'll be fine.

*CLEO looks at their reflection in the mirrors. She pulls the nightgown
up over her shoulders, covering her breasts. At that moment, the door
to the bedroom opens and a boy, eleven, and a girl, nine run in.*

NOAH
Mom, we're hungry.

RUTH
NOAH called me pas intelligent.

NOAH
Or, Tu es stupide. Your choice.

CLEO
*CLEO smiles, puts her arms around the two children and walks out
the door.*

The breakdown of the psyche
begins with small happenstances.

Destruction I
The Memoir

I hated going to the oncologist's office. Much like Pavlov's dog responding to stimuli, my whole essence trembled, making me nauseous as soon as I stepped through the door. I could smell those lethal fumes of chemo, and no matter how friendly and compassionate my nurses were, I disliked them all. They were paid to be pleasant and agreeable.

As I worked up my courage to face the deadly drip once again, I realized my line of defense has weakened. My ability to tune out the nasty, unpleasant, elements of life had become defective. I was not ready to admit this fully. Using techniques I gave to clients on how to push through difficulties, I mustered up enough of a façade to pretend I was strong and capable. With each chemo, I prepared a different plan on how to handle my session, desperately searching for the perfect strategy: Bring a container of herbal tea and drink the mixture throughout the chemo, read jokes and laugh; ingest the holistic medicine for nausea, which I received from a naturopath doctor, meditate and pray. Time and time again, I approached my dilemma with a new angle. Time and time again, I failed.

I will say, some sessions were slightly less deadly than others, my recovery a tiny bit quicker. But the improvement was so slight, it's hardly worth mentioning.

By the time my birthday approached, December 28, 2002, I was extremely sick with a terrible cold. My body blinked frail and thin, as did my spirit. The family vacationed in Anza-Borrego Desert for the winter holidays. On Christmas Eve, while we all sat at a festive table in the dining room, eagerly anticipating a delicious meal, I whispered to my mother-in-law that I felt very sick. I don't want to spoil anyone's good time or have anyone worry about me, so I asked for her advice. She insisted I go to the room and take care of myself.

With trepidation, I excused myself, announcing I needed to rest. I was in exile in my dark, isolated room, which, given the situation, seemed ideal. But comfort and peace really didn't exist there. I felt totally abandoned . . . by my spirit abandoned by my health, abandoned by my once strong, optimistic attitude. Lying down and sleeping was foreign. I thrived on being in the center of life. I died a little death each time I was secluded. I felt miserable and sleep was impossible.

My husband came to the room to check on me. Even in my wretched state, we attempted intimacy. I was determined to keep things as they were—this upstaged my constant suffering from chemo. But my bald scalp, skeletal frame, pale skin were not serving as aphrodisiacs, at least not for me. The life-affirming act of making love did nothing to revitalize my soul. My birthday came and went without my usual *joie de vivre*. New Year's Eve, we went to a party. This usually fulfilled my craving for fun and celebration. But instead found myself standing alone, observing the party protocol. I didn't want to be here I admitted to myself. The noise, the laughter, the merriment assaulted me like a player in a game of dodge ball. Suddenly, I was overcome by exposing, vulnerability. I longed to take refuge inside the safety and comfort of my home. I asked my husband if we could leave. I just didn't feel well. He honored my wishes.

One fact was apparent: I had become more internal. Being around people and existing in the outside world assaulted every one of my senses. I received a gift—a much-needed reprieve thanks to the holidays—no chemo for four weeks. It was now the first week of January 2003 - Time to go to my **last chemo! I HAD NEVER BEEN SO HAPPY!**

My very good friend Sara arrived from Colorado to care for my children and me as I entered my last phase of treatment. Sara brought her camera to the oncologist's office. She took a few pictures of me just before entering through the treatment center doors. A kerchief wrapped around my head, my stomach felt queasy, and already I was dreading the effects of the chemo. Three hours later, the familiar, all-consuming implosion of my body rendered me wailing. I lay on the rug of my walk-in closet and realized how easy it would be to go off the deep-end, never to return. My sanity hovered loosely above me. I could easily jump off the edge at any moment but every ounce of me fought for control. Sara found me in the fetal position, sobbing. "Sheryl, the children want to see you. They want to know you're okay." My outside persona snapped back together, but one foot dangled over the grave's lips.

Part of my psyche was destruction's damage. Part of me will never return. As I left the comfort of my closet that served as a womb-like protection, I dragged my black cloak behind me. *Sheryl was slowly disappearing under this heavy shield.*

CHAPTER 10
Disintegration

Passing, the Movie

INT. KITCHEN IN CLEO'S HOUSE – DAY
CLEO *is talking on the phone.*

CLEO
I'll be there at 1. The Doctor told me it was benign the last time. I'm worried now.

CLEO *listens.*
83 percent accuracy? That leaves a lot of room for mistakes.
(She looks out the kitchen window at the swimming pool. Three blackbirds land on the cement edge of the pool, looking down at the water.)

EXT. – THE SWIMMING POOL

NOAH AND RUTH *burst out of the living room French doors and run on the grass, chasing each other. The birds fly away.*
Noah runs over to the poolside and picks up a black feather and waves it in the air. He yells at his sister.

NOAH
Plume noire. You know what that means? Bad luck. You're going to have bad luck today, Ruth.

RUTH *runs up to him and tries to grab the feather.*

RUTH
It's not a black cat. Black cats bring bad luck.

NOAH *(dangles it over her head.)*

Not in France. A black feather means bad luck in France. The soldiers hated seeing black birds pass over their heads flying, right before they fought a battle. They would say, "Plume noire. C'est dommage."

RUTH
You are such a liar.

NOAH *(hands over the feather to RUTH, but she refuses to take it.)*
Here. Do you want the feather?

RUTH
I don't want it.

NOAH
Why? It's not a chat noir.

RUTH
Stop speaking French! MOOOOM!

INT. KITCHEN

CLEO
I understand nothing is 100 percent accurate.
But it's been a whole year and if something is there, it had all that time to grow.
(She sees RUTH screaming.)

CLEO
Yes. Thank you. Bye.

(CLEO walks brusquely out the kitchen door. She walks up to NOAH and puts out her hand.)

CLEO
Give me the feather. Stop teasing your sister.

NOAH *(looks at the feather and keeps holding it.)*
I'm not teasing her. C'est vrai.

CLEO
Give me the feather, mon petit garçon.

NOAH looks at the feather reluctantly, then hands it over to CLEO.

CLEO drops it to the ground. NOAH watches it fall.

CLEO
Come on you two, time for school.

NOAH and RUTH pass over the feather on the ground and walk with CLEO back into the kitchen.

The human spirit dissolves, even though our physical bodies continue functioning.

Disintegration
The Memoir

The dreadful chemical drip treatment finally completed its course. They gave me a few weeks to regain my energy. It was now time for radiation.

My body felt raw, exposed, torn open by the claws of chemo. And now my right breast would be burned to further destroy any lurking cancer cells. "This will be a piece of cake compared to chemo," the doctor said reassuringly as we sat in his office for a consultation. I grabbed my husband's hand and he squeezed it. I thought to myself, "A piece of cake? I deserve the whole pastry case after what my body's been through!" Of course this doctor has never subjected his body to chemo or radiation. Radiation might also wreak havoc on my body." At this point, I didn't trust what anyone had to say.

I found out I would be spending five days a week for the next seven weeks, receiving radiation treatment at Mission Hospital in Mission Viejo, California. The technicians and I were sure to become fast friends.

The doctor never told me how to care for my breast after it had been radiated in order to prevent burning. I designed a program for myself through my intuition and instincts. An by a wonderful happenstance, a client of mine told her caretaker about my predicament. The nurse was a breast cancer survivor and had treated her radiation burns with a natural gel from an Aloe Vera plant. She kept these plants in her refrigerator and gave the stems to me. I also bought a clay / mud healing powder that I mixed with water, generating a cement-like material that I applied to my breast for drawing out toxins. I was ready to render my body for the next assault.

I established a ritual: Morning time, drive over to the doctor's office. Bring a book for reading in the waiting room to forget about all the damaging side effects. This time, act friendly to the technicians because I felt joy and wanted to do a jig that this was not chemo. I even found some animation in my voice when talking. This is not chemo. This is not chemo. I thought over and over . . . my life is blessed!

I lay down like a lump as the machine targeted the spot for the healing rays. The session was short. Painless as promised. But only if I followed my ministrations immediately at home and not allow the intense rays to obliterate my breast. First I broke open the thick stem of the plant, then stuck my fingers in the soothing substance. With two fingers I rubbed the healing ointment on my breast . . . very cool, very comforting. Next, like an alchemist, I mixed the healing clay with water and covered my breast with the brown, thick, moist mixture. I let it sit on the area for one hour. I reclined on a futon on the floor of the family room, relaxed, and watched television. I'm watched Helen Hunt and Paul Reiser, a couple in the comedy television series *Mad About You*, and it

73

cracked me up. This was exactly what I need emotionally. I was hit by a wave of exhaustion that settled over my body, and I remained there until I had to pick the children up from school at 2:30.

The family room morphed into a protective cave. Day after day for three hours I was alone. I did not interact with anyone. I entered my cocoon of inner silence. The external world blasted my fragile senses and I struggle with the onslaught. I no longer desired to be outside or drive long distances.

Then one day in April the phone rang. I picked it up. "Hi, my name is Diane and I'm your daughter's softball coach."

I broke out in tears. "I've always been my daughter's coach, but I couldn't handle the responsibility because of my radiation treatments." I sobbed uncontrollably, and poor Diane didn't know what to do.

"Well, maybe you can be my assistant coach," she suggested.

The tears stopped. Was I strong enough to handle the task? "Absolutely. I'll help you. We'll make it a winning season."

I could put my longhaired wig into a ponytail just like I used to do with my real hair. Even though I was slowly disintegrating inwardly, I would be damned if I let my daughter down. The game must go on.

CHAPTER 11
Life Passes

Passing, the Movie

EXT. SIDEWALK ON CITY STREET. BOOKSTORE EXTERIOR
– MORNING

CLEO *walks down the street looking at her watch. She passes a
bookstore, and notices a flyer in the window announcing an author
speaking this morning. The title of the lecture catches her eye:
Passing Myself Down to the Grave.*

CLEO *looks at her watch again then decides to enter the bookstore.*

INT. BOOKSTORE.

*People are milling around, waiting for the lecture to begin. Standing
at the edge of the crowd, in the back, is* LEVY. *He's reading a poetry
book.* CLEO *passes by him, knocks into his poetry book, which* LEVY
drops. CLEO *immediately bends down, picks up the book, glances
quickly at its contents, stands, hands the book back to* LEVY. LEVY
takes the book quickly then goes back to reading. CLEO *moves away,
she maneuvers her way down an aisle of seats, passing by people who
already are seated.*

CLEO *passes by* RORY *and his fiancée, and knocks into* RORY'S
knees.

RORY *doesn't notice because* RORY *is intensely whispering into
the girl's ear. The girlfriend nods, then takes out her phone, begins
texting.* RORY *stares off into space, angry.*

CLEO *continues edging down the aisle and sits in a chair at the end.*

MANAGER
Ladies and gentlemen, may I have your attention. Today we are pleased to introduce author, psychotherapist, and breast cancer survivor, Sheryl Aronson, who wrote this compelling memoir, Passing Myself Down to the Grave. Ms. Aronson is a published poet, freelance writer of entertainment and music articles, an aspiring screenwriter, and playwright. She has also been a Marriage, Family Therapist for 25 years in private practice in Laguna Niguel, CA. This is her first published book, although she promises many more to follow. Maybe next time, a novel that she is currently working on called Interview With God. Ladies and Gentlemen, I think you will find Ms. Aronson's talk tonight intriguing as well as inspiring.

SHERYL ARONSON steps up to the podium. She takes a moment to peruse the room allowing her gaze to settle on a few people. She looks directly at CLEO and locks eyes.

CLEO blinks, feels goose bumps rise on her arms, which she rubs unconsciously.

SHERYL places her right hand on the chest area over her left breast and rubs the area with her index and middle finger.

SHERYL
This is where it all began. This is where my psychic wound resides.

(She opens the book and reads.)

I can only speak for myself. But I hope what I've written in this book speaks to you, too, if you suffer, if you lost your way so completely and believe there is no path back to life; if you were thrust into the dark, scary places of your soul by circumstances out of your control; or if you choose to visit this place voluntarily because you think darkness is what you deserve and happiness eludes every step you take. Twelve years ago I was diagnosed with Stage I breast cancer.

CLEO's hands go immediately to the area on her chest. She looks down at her phone and notices the time.

CLEO *(to herself)*
Oh crap . . . gotta go!

She stands up abruptly and rushes out of the bookstore. At the same time RORY'S fiancée says something to him under her breath. He stands and she pushes her way out of the aisle.

RORY waits for a few seconds, breathes heavily, stands then rushes after her. A tall, well-built young boy slides up next to LEVY and pushes his shoulder, making LEVY lose his balance. LEVY looks up startled and THE BOY smiles. THE BOY motions to LEVY they should leave. LEVY follows THE BOY out of the bookstore

SHERYL
The portal to the grave opened...
(She takes a pause. She stares straight ahead.)

Inside of life,
There is another life,
where time stretches backward
and forward endlessly.

Life Passes
The Memoir

2003. My 50th year. My cousin died in July from liver cancer. My chemo and radiation ended by Mother's Day. I took on the responsibility of being an assistant softball coach. I maintained my private practice. I bared my head without a wig in April for the first time, and my hair grew back black, wavy. I had a young boy's cut. I went to Paris for my cousin's memorial. I went to Hawaii for a family vacation in August, planned for my 50th birthday party in December at Dana Point Harbor, wrote original songs for the birthday party and coordinated with my sister's big band to play them. Arranging an instructor for my daughter and her friend to do a dance number for my birthday to "All That Jazz" was another task I took on. I participated in a playwriting class at South Coast Repertory to continue working on my musical. Even though I was busy and seemingly productive, there was a disconnect.

Anxiety plagued my everyday existence. Klonipin, an anti-anxiety drug, removed the edge somewhat, but hyperkinetic waves of nervousness never ceased. I ingested Ambien (a sleeping pill) every night so I could sleep. Dr. Teteff wanted me to take Tomaxaphin for prevention but I refused. I didn't want to put one more drug in my body. I didn't like what the possible side effects were. I was beginning to show bipolar symptoms and my husband was concerned. "You don't sleep, you have these bursts of energy, and get very emotional. Then you withdraw," he told me. "I want you to get checked out for bipolar."

I refused. I knew I wasn't bipolar. I refused to ingest those heavy-duty psychotropic drugs. Although my body moved fast, my mind moved fast, my ability to talk and communicate slowed down. I notice that I had very little to say, which is highly unusual for me because I love to talk. It felt like I was being drained of all of my core spiritual beliefs and practices. It felt like there wasn't one original thought left in my head . . . then suddenly I had an astonishing thought: "I've said everything I needed to say in this lifetime."

One night I noticed as I sat in a friend's living room listening to everyone's conversations, I reached deep inside myself trying to find something to contribute to the conversation. Only a blank space appeared. From then on, anything that came out of my mouth was forced . . . unnatural.

How could I explain what was going on with me? I didn't die of the breast cancer . . . at least not yet, but I realized a huge void within my psyche, and a part of me died. Nothing I could do or say filled this hole. Nothing erased the hysterical anxiety that raced around my system. I reverted back to my old coping skills. I continued to be the busy, productive, seemingly open and friendly, loquacious mother, wife, therapist, and friend.

I wrote a song for my 50th birthday called "Going Home" about where I was headed next in my life, as I honored and passed through the memorable year of 50. But the words from my song foreshadowed something much more sinister. Four years later, I took pills and drank Tequila, trying to go home.

CHAPTER 12
Life Passes

Passing, the Movie

INT. EXAMINING ROOM OF DOCTOR'S OFFICE.

CLEO sits alone in a chair of an examining room staring at the door. The door opens and the technician and radiologist walk in.

RADIOLOGIST *(laughing)*
I couldn't believe my luck. A hole-in-one on the 18th.

TECHNICIAN
You're always lucky. No four-leaf clovers for you. Save them for us unlucky ones.

CLEO
(Looks at both with a frown on her face.)
Excuse me. I'm waiting for my results.

RADIOLOGIST
Yes, sorry Mrs. Lionne. You must go to the hospital at once and get a biopsy on this lump. The results of your mammogram came back problematic. We have to look at the biopsy to see if there are cancer cells present. Right now it looks very suspicious.

CLEO
(Looks dumbfounded.)
You're kidding. A biopsy? Why the rush? Can't I go another day when my husband is available? It took you a whole year to determine this. Are you kidding me?

RADIOLOGIST
I am recommending you do it now. You shouldn't wait. I'll call the

the hospital and get you in.
(He walks out.)

TECHNICIAN
I'm really sorry. Is there anything I can do for you?

CLEO
How about changing the results.

TECHNICAN
(Laughs nervously.)
Wouldn't that be great! Are you all right?

CLEO
Not any better than before. Will the biopsy hurt?

TECHNICIAN
Not too much. They freeze the area . . . some stinging and pinching,
maybe. You'll be fine.

CLEO
Really . . .

TECHNICIAN
(Walks to the door.)
Good luck.
(Walks out the door.)

CLEO
(Once again stares at the door.

Doors close. And all I could do was watch them shut.

Doors Close
The Memoir

2003 rushed to a close. My actual birthday, December 28, fell on a Saturday night. The party room at Dana Point Harbor looked very festive. Tiny, sparkly lights were hung around the room. The color theme was black and white with a buffet of delicious food awaiting the partygoers. My sister's big band, The Great American Swing Band, was setting up in the corner to entertain. A decorated Christmas tree was at the entrance, greeting guests as they walked through the doors. People affectionately placed their gifts under the tree.

There were 40 adults and my two children and their three friends. Three of my very closest friends came from all over the world just to be here for me, flying in from Sedona, Arizona, Trinidad, Colorado, and Paris, France. I was surrounded by love and happiness. I chose a winter green gown for the evening. Because my hair was still short, I passed on going to the salon. I wore a natural style in my natural hair color Cleopatra Black with miniature curls forming on the top. I was a reedy size 8 to my 5'8" frame, and yes, utterly delighted; never in my life had I been this skinny. At 50, this was what I wanted.

For the first song, I requested that my sister's band perform "Who Cares About Me?" This number was the closing song in the First Act of my musical, *On the Road to Your Heart*. The piece was arranged by a talented jazz bass player, and was the perfect melody for that big band sound. Originally I saw this song as a lament, then as a triumphant realization for every single woman who was looking for love. The rhythm was upbeat with an animated chorus number at the end. The tone of the song was somewhat sarcastic but hopeful.

The first lines of the song:
I knew I had to face it
Sooner or later
Why couldn't I see...
That the men I was choosing to be my lovers
Weren't right for me.
My heart's been broken into a million pieces
Will I ever repair
My trust again in finding love
Or am I doomed to despair?
My friends say
You choose a certain type
Who doesn't care about me.
He tells me if I fuss or gripe
He won't care about me.
I love each man with my entire life
You'd think he'd care about me.
The time has come to find Mr. Right
Who cares about me?

***

I had found Mr. Right. At the age of 36, I married for the second time. I put in my request to the universe just before my 35th birthday on Christmas Day. I said the following: God, I am ready to meet my husband. I am ready to become a wife, have children, and establish myself as a psychotherapist in private practice. Lo and behold on January 1st, I had my first date with my husband.

That date turned into a whole weekend, then a half-year courting period. That July he asked me to marry him. And on April 16, 1989, I was married. I moved from Los Angeles to Laguna Niguel. Strangely enough, I had told one of the detectives at the Anaheim Police Station (I worked as a counselor for adolescents that committed minor infractions against the law) that I would never move to Orange County in order to be closer to work. I have now lived in Orange County longer than anywhere else.

I created a private practice where I also taught seminars on women's self-esteem and relationships. In 1992, my son was born, and in 1994 . . . my daughter. The house we lived in overlooked Saddleback Valley, our master bedroom ran the whole length of the top floor with a huge walk-in closet and balcony out the side door. We found it when I was pregnant with my daughter and knew instantly it is the one we wanted to live in with our new family. Our Psychology Practice is located just down the hill in Town Center, making my mothering tasks convenient. I can work a few hours, take care of the children then go back in the evening. Like Job in the Bible (before he lost everything), my life was flourishing. I had everything my heart and soul needed.

But as I stood in the center of my life, 14 years later at my 50th birthday celebration on December 28, 2003, I no longer felt so safe and secure. A dark, hollow space seemed to take over my inner being with a void that offered no real future. Now for my second song . . .

My professional, guitar-playing friend informed me that I was to perform with him on "Coming Home." So I boldly belted out the lyrics, slightly off-key. That song revealed all my experiences that brought me here to this meaningful place. I was coming home.

I'd reached a dead end. After my party, I silently unraveled. It was so swift, so insane, and any steps I took to recover the old me evaporated. I didn't dare reveal my secrets that I no longer wanted to live in our gorgeous home; I didn't want to be an upstanding wife, mother, or professional anymore, either. I didn't want to be tied down to anyone or anything. I just wanted to be an irresponsible adolescent, wild and free!

My adult self knew acting like this was dangerous and completely out of control, but that part of me wasn't strong enough to exert any kind of authority. Something bigger than me took over and started my descent into darkness, shutting the doors to life as I had once lived it.

CHAPTER 13
More Doors Closing

Passing, the Movie

INT.BEDROOM -NIGHT

RORY and his girlfriend LAURA are making love in her bed. She is on top moving her body slowly, teasingly, whispering to him. RORY reaches up to grab her and bring LAURA close. SHE avoids his hands, laughs, and continues her sexual play. Suddenly RORY throws LAURA off of him, and jumps out of bed.

LAURA
What's wrong with you?

RORY
You, that's what's wrong.
(He takes his pants and puts them on.)

LAURA
Me? You love to be teased, tempted.

RORY
You just want to be in control. I allowed it. No more.
(He grabs his shirt and puts it on.)

LAURA
(Jumps out of bed, stands in front of RORY, blocking his way.)
You're fucked up. You don't know what you want. You change your mind every day.

RORY
Not about you.

LAURA
What do you mean?

RORY
(Reaches inside his pants pocket and takes out a small jewelry case. He opens the box and a diamond ring is inside.)

LAURA
(Gasps. Stares at the ring, then slowly reaches for it.)

RORY
(He grabs her hand and gets down on one knee.)

LAURA
(Lifts him up gently so he's standing in front of her.)
Now... RORY.

RORY
LAURA, marry me. Be with me forever.

LAURA
Are you sure?

RORY
Shit.
(He makes a move to break away from her, LAURA holds tightly onto him.)

LAURA
Okay, Babe. Yes. Now let's get back to bed.
(SHE turns her back on him, and walks back to the bed.)

RORY
(Still holding the ring, walks over to the bed and holds it out to LAURA. She puts her hand out and he slips it on the ring finger. He takes off his shirt, his pants, and then climbs on top of her. Their love making resumes.)

There were warning signs.
I didn't understand them.

More Doors Closing
The Memoir

Planning my son's Bar Mitzvah is top priority. Neil was turning 13 in February 2005.

In the spring of 2004, my inner self crumbled as I frantically tried to put the pieces back together. I sat with my husband in the elegant art-deco style restaurant, test tasting the food for the upcoming Bar Mitzvah party. I thought, "I might not even be married at the time this event happens." However, as soon as the idea popped into my mind, I immediately shoved it out with, "What the hell are you thinking? Your life is wonderful, fulfilling, productive, full of love!"

These words were slowly manifesting as I tried to convince myself to stay put. I was wrestling daily with this new demon. I didn't care if my husband and I took separate vacations. I didn't care if I stayed out late at a girlfriend's house, talking past midnight. I didn't care if I acted out recklessly. A part of me was aching to be free. As a therapist, I knew better. It was time for counseling.

I ignored the thought. I was on a self-destructive path of which I had no control. This dark force existed and drove me to the deep, dark depths of my psyche.

Satan rubbed his hands together with a smirk on his face, looking up to God. "She won't survive this undertaking. Without having access to your goodness, she's destroyed."

God shakes his head then patiently replies, "I am never lost to her. I have told Sheryl that I would take everything away from her but I will always be there, even if this happened."
Satan glares at God as if he was left out of some secret. "When… when did you tell her these things?"

With infinite patience and love God replies, "In dreams, dear angel, in dreams."

The Prophetic Dreams:

I woke up sobbing. It was the morning of the Harmonic Conversion, August 17, 1987. My heart felt like it had been ripped from my chest, creating an exposed portal to sorrow. Waves of sadness gushed through me, and I just couldn't stop crying. "What's wrong?" my boyfriend Roger asked helplessly. We were in Cape Cod, visiting my parents at their summer home, rented for the month of August. "God took everything away from me." I began to cry. The images flew by so quickly, I couldn't grasp any of them, but I remembered being emptied of all my possessions. My soul was left empty, and I ached from being so exposed and vulnerable.

"What do you mean?" he asked puzzled.

I was too hysterical to explain . . . and I really didn't understand the dream. However, the one precious creature I loved more than anything else at the time was our cat Kidder (or Face as I used to call her), and God did not take her away from me. A bit of relief from that fact eased the severe aching I was feeling inside. Like all dreams, the heartbreak and pain faded as the day progressed, and I soon forgot about the terror I had experienced upon awakening. A few weeks later (Labor Day Weekend), my boyfriend ended our two-year relationship with a curt, Dear John letter. He had met someone else. But at least he didn't take Kidder; he knew how much I loved her. My aunt died from cancer that very same weekend. She was my mother's sister and much like a second mother to me. She was also the mother of my dear cousin Bob. I think the dream had come true because I had lost two very important relationships.

After the grief subsided, I forgot the dream. My first date with my husband -to -be was January 1, 1988.

"Why do you bother?" Satan asked God. "Humans don't understand. They forget about your existence. They allow me to tempt them and lead their souls into the hell of their existence on earth. They forsake you."

"Without you, dear angel, they would never know me in all my glory."

"Huh?"

"I create all my beloveds for a reason, you're no exception."

"I'm not through with her."

"I know."

Four dreams complete the cycle.
In December 1992, my husband and I journeyed to Israel for two weeks with our nine-month old son. The season was Hanukkah, and we were in the country where religion originated. I felt the presence of God so strongly, and my entire being vibrated with a visceral sense of Adonai's presence. The air around me smelled sweetly sacred as God's land caressed my soul. The dreams started as soon as we arrived.

94

I'd awaken each time with a peaceful heart and wonderment, realizing something significant was happening.   Yet, I had no idea why.

Dream One: I was standing on a stage naked, and the people in the audience were clapping loudly. I couldn't figure out why everyone is applauding me, and I felt very vulnerable being so exposed. Yet, I stood there and didn't run off the stage.

Dream Two: I was sitting on top of a palm tree and God's voice said to me, "Sheryl, if I wanted to throw you on top of the other palm tree over there. . . I could do it, because I AM GOD! I looked over to the palm tree across my way and wondered how God could make this happen, but I believed the words spoken to me.

Dream Three: I was sitting on an airplane and noticed the plane was heading toward an apartment building. At that moment I thought to myself, "This is it. Prepare to die." Then God split the apartment in half like the Red Sea, and the airplane flew through it safely.

Dream Four: It was the end of the world. Chaos and war erupted all around me, and I was hiding in the corner, behind a table, protecting my head. I heard in the heavens, "Look up to the sky Sheryl." I gaze upward and the clouds radiated golden pink rays. God spoke to me, "No matter what happens around you, I am always here."

Satan tugs on God's arm. "She never understood those dreams. In the darkest hour, she was convinced you abandoned her. Like all humans, Sheryl showed weakness and chose to go down to the grave when you were lost to her. Humph!"

"It's all part of the plan, Dear Angel."

Satan glares at God and points his finger. "You and your grand design. Humans always screw up whatever blessings you bestow upon them. Why don't you just give up and let me run the show?"

"Remember my first book I gave to mankind?"

95

"THE BOOK OF JOB. You mystified the Rabbis because they couldn't figure out where this story originated, and how it related to the Old Testament. Even the wisest of men were baffled by your actions." With the most beguiling of smiles, Satan tries to charm God one more time. "Put me in charge. Man understands me much better than you."

"Maybe you're right."

"What?"

"Time to step back . . ."

"Huh?"

"You do come up with good ideas."

Satan frowns. "I do?"

"You know, Sheryl passed herself down to the grave. She's rising again."

"What do you mean I have good ideas? You actually listen to me?"

"Always, dark one, always."

In October of 2004, I slammed the door to my marriage and walked into a threshold of despair. Chaos erupted like a volcano inside my mind and the molten lava of confusion sprayed out of every one of my pores. Helplessly, I walked away from my dream relationship and family; my dream house and job. I turned my back on everything I had asked God to give me 14 years ago in my prayer just as I turned 35.

A wild, petrified adolescent girl emerged who demanded attention and turned a deaf ear to the adult-me trying to reason with her. My ability to access the psychological skills and spiritual practices I had cultivated over 30 years was now non-existent.

CHAPTER 14
A Wild Fire Burning Inside

Passing, the Movie

INT. BOOKSTORE – AFTERNOON

(LEVY sits at a table in the coffee shop writing in a notebook. He sips his coffee, thinks, and writes some more. A tall, muscular boy of 18 sits down at LEVY'S table and slaps his hand down on the paper.)

BRIAN
Writing me love poetry again?

LEVY
(Stares at BRIAN'S hand. He remains silent.)

BRIAN
Let me see what the brilliant boy has written today.
(He grabs the notebook and reads out loud . . .)
Passing, The river flows over my feet.
Ancient waters reveal no wisdom.
What bullshit brilliant boy. What the fuck does this mean?

LEVY
Nothing. It means nothing.

BRIAN
(Continues reading.)
I am empty to the bottom,
Like a dry vessel
Cracked
Broken
Deep mother fucka . . . deep.

LEVY
(Shakes his head and tries to grab the notebook back. BRIAN smacks his hand away and glares at him.)

BRIAN
I'm trying to get educated here. You're way over my head geek-bitch.

LEVY
(Crosses his arms over his chest).

BRIAN
(Ignores him and continues reading.)
A gun speaks my truth.
Bullets blast salvation.
A boy's body
Rests at peace.
Passing through existence
No more.

(BRIAN looks LEVY in the eyes.)
You don't have the balls to do this.

LEVY
My balls are my business.

BRIAN
I'm sure you'd like to make them mine.

LEVY
(Grabs for the notebook and the page rips that the poem was written on. LEVY stuffs the notebook in his backpack. He stands up.)

BRIAN
Leaving me lover boy? Gonna go shoot yourself?

(LEVY stalks away.)

(BRIAN watches him leave then stretches out his legs and smiles).

Like Levy,
I attempted to use writing
to understand my dilemma.

A Wild Fire Burning Inside
The Memoir

December 23, 2006
My anxiety set in. I started breathing heavy, panting, and fear crept into my heart like a viper – then a voice said, "I will rinse my coffee cup. I will fill up the glass with water. I will take my vitamins. I will call my sister. I will! I will! I will!" Little tasks that eased the panic were essential. I sat and meditated then heard, "You have the tools to fight – to change your inner turmoil – to transform your life. Remember to surrender to God and trust that there is a Divine Plan." Why did the future that I created, and was always so clear, look like nothing now?

January 1, 2007
My grownup side barely existed. She knew how to drive, she could do some daily tasks, and the children seemed more responsible. She was protesting, not wanting to do much, and she felt weak, helpless. It was important for me to survive, to live life out. It was important for me to survive for my children.

May 24, 2007

I couldn't find anything inside myself, so I kept running. I truly needed to face my inner terror. I felt empty. There were no answers. I had no power, but all these negatives just contributed to more negatives. I didn't see a future, and that's what was so scary. I didn't know what I wanted, or what I was even capable of so I kept going back and forth. I felt so alone, so disconnected with no words, and nothing to say, except the same old thing. How could I break free and continue? There were times when I thought I could feel and see an answer, but when it came right down to it, I couldn't honor that answer . . . around and around I went

---

Satan rubs his hands together obsessively, and then licks his lips as if savoring a delicious meal. "No soul, hee, hee . . . she was so lost – yes, lost . . . hee hee, no glory, no light, no God. I had a field day with her.

God nods. "You did."

Satan raises his left leg then his right leg and his feet stomp the ground. His arms swing wildly in a crazed dance. "I won! I won!" His victory cry permeates the air.

"Like Job, she beseeched me, dear Angel."

But Satan hears nothing as he continues his dance.

May 24, 2007 (Continued)

My journey through the night remained dark and scary; yet I had to keep walking and thank God for another day for being alive. Somewhere deep inside myself there was a knowing and steadfastness. I needed to find a way back to me. I needed to see the beauty in life and the beauty in myself.

June 20, 2007

If there was a place inside of me that could feel happiness, confidence, I pleaded to be allowed to reach down and find it.

From the moment I ended my marriage, despair and anxiety crushed my spirit. So many forces acosted me. So many confusing thoughts danced around like a Mexican jumping bean. I wanted to go back to my family, back to the safety and security of my life, but a stronger, more devious energy controlled the dance. Each new day mocked me, threatening my survival. All I could do was put one foot in front of the other.

I rented a three-bedroom townhouse that looked like a miniature replica of the home I had left behind. I decided that house belonged to my husband and the children, not me. It's their home and I needed to find my own home. I had helped decorate that property, and over the years my husband and I added art ceramics from artisans. I felt those possessions no longer belonged to me. I left my home and all its exquisiteness, as if I'd been running from a fire, forced to leave all my worldly possessions behind in exchange for my own survival. And now . . . I was homeless and soulless.

We had joint custody of the kids, and I attempted to give my son and daughter all the love, protection, and guidance I could possibly muster. But a wild, adolescent girl was really running the show, and I was a scared woman who was wretched, lost, and full of desolation. I wore the mask of mother the best I could. All my coping mechanism evaporated, leaving me void of any and all of my former years of experience of psychological or spiritual skills. Every technique, every meditation or chanting session could not penetrate the insane desperation that was drowning my soul. I went to metaphysical healers. I went to Buddhist meetings. I wrote. I talked with friends. I put myself on anti-depressants and anti-anxiety drugs. I reached into my big bag of tricks, but I failed at every attempt.

On the outside I looked fantastic, I was slim, physically fit, my hair's natural curls grew out after the chemo and crowned my head with sweet ringlets that I dyed strawberry blonde. I experienced manic energy at times which exploded into a full-blown episode, so I stopped taking my anti-depressants.

I didn't consult a psychiatrist when I did this. It was the summer of 2008 when Barack Obama announced his candidacy for President. I decided I wanted to organize a fundraiser for him and started attending meetings for the Democratic party around Orange County. At this time my personality was too assertive and overbearing. The children backed away from me and my friends began to worry. I was loud, opinionated, and bossy, but I felt I was accomplishing something. I decide to donate money to Obama's campaign and attended a fundraiser for him in Newport Beach. I shook his hand and I took pictures.

The summer, and into the winter of 2008, marked my last big blast of happiness and creativity before the darkness of my soul took over, completely wiping out my internal light. However, God was still guiding me in ways that still reveal themselves today as I look back, writing this memoir. The saying, "God works in mysterious ways" is absolutely true.

CHAPTER 15
The Guiding Hand of God

Passing, the Movie

INT. DOWNSTAIRS BATHROOM IN CLEO'S HOUSE –EARLY MORNING

(CLEO stands half-naked, breasts exposed, looking into the mirror. She takes her hair and puts it on top of her head, then covers it with her hands, determining how she would look with no hair. For a brief moment she sees LEVY and RORY'S faces in the mirror, looking back at her. CLEO is startled. She drops her hair, pulls up her pajama top and walks into the adjoining den. She approaches and scans the bookshelf for books. CLEO reaches for a book, takes it off the shelf then opens up the book randomly to a page. She gasps. On the page, she sees a white bird flying out of a cage. Suddenly the door to the den opens and her husband walks in.)

DANIEL
Trouble sleeping again, honey? (He looks at the book) What you got there?

CLEO
(Shuts the book.) I think it's a sign.

DANIEL
A sign? What kind of sign?

CLEO
Everything is going to be okay.

DANIEL
(He reaches out and hugs her.)

DANIEL *(Cont ...)*
I know you're worried about the surgery next week, but you'll be fine.
I know what a fighter you are. You never give up. Besides, the kids
and I all need you.

CLEO
(Kisses DANIEL on the cheek)
I know. Go back to sleep. I'm going to stay here a while longer.

DANIEL
(Hugs her again.)
You'll be okay.

CLEO
(Pulls out of his embrace and sits on the couch with the book in hand.)

DANIEL
(Yawns. Stretches.)
Long day ahead tomorrow. Non-stop clients.

CLEO
Go back to sleep sweetheart.

DANIEL
Night. (Walks out the door.)

CLEO
(Stretches out on the couch with the book on her chest. She closes her
eyes.)

DREAM SEQUENCE

EXT. RIVER –DAYTIME

LEVY's dead body floats in the water.

Cut to:
EXT. WOODS – DAYTIME

RORY hangs by the noose, dead.

Cut to:
EXT. SWIMMING POOL – DAYTIME

CLEO bursts out of the water in a swimming pool as a white bird flies overhead.

INT. DEN – EARLY MORNING

CLEO sits up abruptly. The book falls to the floor. She cries.

God's presence and love illuminates
the darkest corners of my soul,
which makes sense of a message,
determined by one's state of mind.

The Guiding Hand of God
The Memoir

Although anxiety plagued my very existence on a daily basis, I
hid my feelings well. I decided to look for a job and got hired
by a Managed Health Care Insurance Company that used
psychotherapists to do intakes, and then refer patients to a local
therapist in their area. While there, I became friends with the
only other female therapist on staff and gave her some advice
about traveling to Paris. Her name was Susan. My story with
her comes back later.

I only lasted six weeks at this position because I became personally involved with the assistant of the company's president, helping her with her drinking problem. I was fired for knowing intimate details and inside knowledge regarding the company. At that time I was also thrilled about Obama being the Democratic candidate for the race of Presidency, and decided to organize a fundraiser in Orange County to help his cause. I networked with a predominantly African American Baptist church in Irvine; I attended other political events. I volunteered at the Democratic Headquarters in Laguna Beach, and I found a new group of friends who were involved in the same cause. I even wrote a song to play at my fundraiser called "The Democratic Boogie," which my sister's swing band plays. I also arranged for a dance troupe from the Baptist church to perform the song.

When I learned Barack Obama was coming to Newport Beach for a fundraiser, I donated money to meet the man in person. I just knew he was going to be someone special. I stood anxiously before a taped-off area in a ballroom with an Instamatic camera in my hands, ready to shoot this very auspicious occasion.

Obama entered the room like a prince, smiling and gracious. Everyone rushed to shake his hand. I snapped as many pictures as possible with my cheap camera. When he walked by me, I held out my hand. He shook it and I told him, "My cousin Noam Scheiber has interviewed you (he writes for a magazine in Washington D.C.). Mr. Obama replied very friendly, "Your cousin is a good writer," then moved forward to his next guest. The night President Obama was elected, I was working behind the bar at the Democratic Headquarters in Laguna Beach. I partied with all the ecstatic Democrats down in South County. My son and my ex-husband (with his now girlfriend) were there as well.

Temporarily, I was high on life. But I had no job. I was living moment to moment with whatever appealed to me at the time. My boyfriend constantly told me that I was acting too boldly; I was too hyper, too assertive for him. I had no plans. My anxious, nervous energy penetrated every cell of my body and propelled me into a frenzied orbit of creative yet out of control excitement with a bevy of sporadic projects.

I sought guidance from a woman who was a spiritual counselor. No matter what she recommended, I couldn't calm myself down. One day while sitting in my car after I left a session, I heard a voice in my head. "Sheryl, you need to go to your Jewish Temple." I was shocked and wondered why I was hearing this instruction. But I did as I was commanded and drove to Temple Beth-el in Aliso Viejo. I walked upstairs to the hall where the services were held, and when I entered, I saw an artist painting an exquisite landscape of old Jerusalem on a large backdrop wall. My mouth hung open. I had been guided here for a reason. I hadn't been to my Temple since my daughter was Bat Mitvahed. I quietly watched the artist paint then asked him what he was doing. He replied, "I was hired by the Temple to paint Jerusalem back in the olden days, but I had no idea what to paint. Then I had a dream and this was my vision: There's a brick wall in the foreground and a path along the wall. Part of the painting exists in light. Then there is the path running to the left where one enters into darkness within a house . . . as if one is walking into a cave."

I asked him to explain the meaning behind the light and the darkness.

"Man starts in the light when he is born, at the beginning of his life . . . He continues on his journey, and at some point man must walk through the dark night of his soul, which is represented here as the door to this house, shadowed in darkness."

My heart raced because his story reflected everything I was going through. As we talked more, I learned about his life, told him what had just happened to me regarding losing my job. When I told him where I had worked, we discovered that Susan, the other female therapist who asked me about Paris, was one of his best friends.

I know God guided me here for a reason. I understood his painting with my soul, and felt encouraged by the synchronicity of the circumstances. I decided to find the Rabbi.

I believed my life was echoing Job's story. I found him and he invited into his office, offering me a seat. "Rabbi, can you please tell me about THE BOOK OF JOB."

"Well, Sheryl, no one knows where this story came from. It's a mystery that the scholars have been trying to solve throughout the years. But we do know it has always been a separate story that is not tied to the rest of the Old Testament." He then handed me his Bible. "Here, you take this and keep it."

I was honored that the Rabbi gave me his holy book. But I put it away and never read the story. I carried the Bible around with me for years, never ever opening the book. Until just recently in May 2014. Once again God revealed to me how I am living THE BOOK OF JOB. My revelation will be told at the end.

CHAPTER 16
Without Hope

Passing, the Movie

INT. KITCHEN – DAY TIME
(LEVY is sitting at the kitchen table doing his homework. His mother runs into the room.)

MOTHER
I'm so screwed.

LEVY
Mom. What's wrong?

MOTHER
I'm late again for work.

LEVY
Maybe you shouldn't go out partying all the time at night. Rest some.

MOTHER
(She takes LEVY'S face in her hands and kisses him)
My studious son, always looking out for his mother.
(She notices he has a black eye.)
What's with the eye?

LEVY
Nothing.

MOTHER
Really?

LEVY
Soccer ball hit me in the eye.

MOTHER
(Looks quizzically at him. Looks at her watch)

Damn. Gotta run son.
(She jolts out the door)
(The phone rings.)

LEVY
Yeah.
BRIAN
I see your mother's gone.

LEVY
(Says nothing)

BRIAN
Well lover boy, I'm coming over.

LEVY
(Hangs up. Writes in his notebook)

No more answers are available.
A showdown is inevitable.

Without Hope
The Memoir

My boyfriend and I return from our Christmas in Paris. The trip was perfect. We spent Christmas Eve with my friend Aline, her husband, and her immediate family. I felt alive, connected, exhilarated. Paris sparkled with its usual erotic and cultural energy in which I immersed myself.

The trip abroad distracted me from my lack of purpose. I had no direction. I had absolutely no idea who I was, or how I was supposed to move forward in a career, in a relationship, and inside myself. One month later, I attempted suicide.

In January 2009, after both of my children left for school (my son was in high school, my daughter, junior high), I sat on my couch in the living room thinking, "Now what?" I felt empty. I felt lost. I saw no future. I convinced myself that I had done everything I wanted to do in my life and there was nothing more to do or to say. A bottle of Klonopin sat on my coffee table, taunting at me. I picked up the bottle of pills, walked to the sink, poured a glass of water, and swallow them all.

I lay down on the couch in the living room with the television on, and the last thing I remembered thinking was, "I just want to sleep and not feel any pain." When I woke up eight hours later, my ex-husband and my boyfriend were in my living room staring down at me. My children had packed their suitcases and were heading out the door to go back to their father's house. Both men took me to the emergency room at the local hospital. And after an examination, I was promptly escorted in an ambulance and whisked away to the Psych ward of the very hospital where I gave birth to my two children.

I had treated patients in this very ward and knew people on staff. Now I was the patient! And the terror of being locked up struck me so profoundly that I nearly fainted. All I wanted to do was get out of this prison. Yes . . . I needed treatment. But I didn't care. I wanted my freedom. The freedom to try to kill myself again.

I knew the system. I was a respected therapist in the community and knew the staff. The psychiatrist granted me a release to my boyfriend after one and a half days of lockup as long as I gave the hospital the name of a doctor I agreed to see for treatment, tell them the date of my scheduled appointment, then promise I would stay with someone who could watch over me. I agreed to all their terms.

I tried to kill myself three more times. Each attempt more serious than the one prior; I was determined, but so was God. I wanted to die. God had other plans for me. Inside my soul, existed a dark void, and asI screamed for help, only silence echoed back.

Much like my dream in 1987 when God took everything away from me, I was unable to access the ability to heal myself. It felt like God had banished my being and my capacity to hope or love; and like Job, I saw no reason to live. The war for my soul continued. I was a mortally wounded soldier, marching down to the grave, praying for peace from all the psychic pain that raced throughout my body and mind. The Sheryl who existed for over 50 years had no home, no resting place, no connection to anything familiar, no peace, no laughter, no memories of happiness and safety. I passed myself off as a ghost who wandered into the pit of despair.

Satan leers at God. His beatific smile saccharinely permeates the air, causing the angels to sweat. God lovingly wipes each of their brows then kisses the Angels on the forehead. Satan rushes over to the end of the line awaiting his kiss. God lifts Satan's face and tilts it up to heaven. "Although Sheryl believes I have deserted her, I exist everywhere and am always there, loving and protecting her. This is the promise I made."

Satan laughs. "She knows nothing. She is weak. She is defeated. She's heading down to the grave, never to rise again. I win."

"For now, dear angel, for now."

The hospital in Laguna Beach released me to my boyfriend who reassured them I would stay at his house so he could help me recover. I convinced everyone I wouldn't hurt myself again. I lied. Meanwhile, I felt disorientated, dead inside, and began isolating myself from my friends. A few weeks passed and this hollow feeling kept growing. When my boyfriend left for a business trip to Arizona, the urge to go to sleep and never wake up took over. I opened my bottle of Ambien, grabbed a bottle of tequila from the refrigerator, and swallowed every pill. I phoned my boyfriend. "I just took a whole bottle of sleeping pills with tequila. I'm so sorry but I can't take it anymore . . . The dogs are safe outside." I dozed off on the couch.

My eyes flew open. The obnoxious, fluorescent lights attacked my vision. My arms, resting on a soft blanket were stuck with tubes. They had placed a catheter placed inside me to urinate, and it assaulted my every move. My throat was parched. I wore a skimpy hospital gown with my bare legs cold and exposed. I was not dead.

A hand grabbed mine and squeezed it. It was my sister. She hovered over me and was deeply concern.

"Why did you do this?" she asked with pain in her voice.
I said nothing. My reasons made sense to me, but how could I describe to her the unbearable psychic pain that was terrorizing my soul?

"I've arranged for you to be admitted to a Psych hospital in Valencia instead of the State hospital here in West Covina. You wouldn't like the one here, trust me. I talked the staff into releasing you into my care as long as I promised to drive you to the hospital."

Dread invaded my body. I didn't want to be locked up again. I couldn't bear the reality of not having my freedom. Being in the hospital under someone's watch all the time made me ill.

My sister continued, "So you get dressed and I'm taking you there now."

I inched on my clothes. A nurse helped detach all the hospital instruments and brought me a wheel chair, lowering my body into it. The whole time I was hatching a plan to escape. Sitting in the backseat of my sister's car, I watched the night sky zoom by, and the cold, hard road of the freeway beckoned me. I envisioned opening the back car door and rolling out so the other vehicles could run over my body. My sister nervously turned around to check on me. I touched the door, experimenting. "What are you doing?" Raising her voice. "You're not thinking about opening

118

the back door!" I backed away. After an hour drive, we arrived at the hospital. As I waited my turn to be called for intake, my mind was racing with ideas: "What kind of disturbed person is going to be my roommate. How will I go to bed early? I need sleeping pills to fall asleep. What happens if I can't or never fall asleep? What kind of meds will they give me? How do I get out of here?"

"Sheryl Aronson, come with me." A woman called from the doorway. My sister hugged me goodbye. I watched her turn away and walk out the door to freedom. A tidal wave of tears flowed through me, but not ONE TEAR fell from my eyes. I was now officially 51/50. I was a danger to myself. Until I proved otherwise, I would be locked up.

CHAPTER 17
Locked In a Dungeon

Passing, the Movie

EXT. A PATIO OUTSIDE A HOUSE – NIGHT

RORY picks up engagement ring from the ground. He turns it over and over in his hand. He looks at the dark window. Everything around him looks bleak and barren. He takes off his belt and ties a noose with it. Slips it over his throat. A light goes on for a second. He looks up with hope. But then it shuts off again. He pulls the belt tighter around his throat. The door opens suddenly.

LAURA
RORY...STOP!

RORY
(Quickly loosens the belt around his neck.)
Talk to me.

LAURA
I've said everything.

RORY
I know you love me.
(He thrusts the ring toward her. LAURA stares at it for a moment tempted... then she gently closes his fist and pushes his arm back toward him.)

LAURA
I can't. Your love is unquenchable.

RORY
(He bends his head to his chin.)
I know.

LAURA
It's how you approach life... that's why I love you.
That's why I can't marry you. (She turns and goes back into the house.
The light blinks off.)

RORY
(Throws the ring into the darkness. Walks away with belt hanging
from his neck.)

I am locked away
in my own misery.

Locked In a Dungeon
The Memoir

Books. I requested my boyfriend bring me books to pass the time while locked up in the psych ward. Morning, noon, and night I read voraciously, losing myself in the stories. My fingers turned the pages one after the other, caressing the smooth texture of the paper as my mind took in every word. I was no longer Sheryl, but a mental patient, locked in a dungeon. I had became a heroine sleighing dragons with a mighty sword.

Reality. Morning. My eyes opened. Shit. I'm still here. Locked up. My chest filled with remorse. A nurse walked in.

"Time to take your blood pressure." Mine was always perfect. What to wear? Don't care. I only possessed a handful of clothes brought to me by my boyfriend.

Exercise. Before breakfast I went to the dining room to work out. Why? Didn't want to gain weight while I was locked up. All day long I sat around either in a counseling group or watching television. I wanted to convince the staff I was mentally healthy so my release would come sooner than later. Dread pushed down on my entire body, moment to moment as I stretched.

Breakfast. A menu was handed out every morning in order to choose our meals for the rest of the day. My head hurt with indecision, too many choices. On one hand I didn't want to eat anything. My stomach cringed at the sight of food. On the other hand I wanted to eat all the desserts to give myself some pleasure. I chose the healthy fare.

Circled the main dish, circled the drink, and circled the dessert, small circles filled up a sheet day after day, determining how I would fill my belly. I dreaded each morning, making my circle of choices.

Yes or No. The same question asked every day. "Do I still want to hurt myself?" The answer was Yes. I told the kind psychiatrist, "No." All I wanted to do was get the hell out of here! Being locked up was even worse than all the psychic pain that attacked my inner being. I knew what to say to give the impression I was improving. I smiled. I actively participated in the groups and told my story. "I had breast cancer. After the chemo and radiation treatments my life was never the same. I went crazy. I left my marriage. I couldn't work. I couldn't sleep." The therapist leading the group nodded her head. I was just reciting words. I wasn't connected to any of it . . . or to any emotion. I felt nothing. Uttering sentences felt like I was dragging heavy blocks of cement one by one across a road.

"You need to be here for two weeks," the psychiatrist told me. I gulped. I nodded my head. "The staff is very concerned that you are at high risk of hurting yourself." I fooled no one. "But if you want to petition this decision, we can schedule a date for a hearing." I asked for a hearing.

Talking on the phone. Quarters were needed to make phone calls so my boyfriend had to supply this precious currency. What to say? What to say to my children? "Mommy is okay. I love you." These words were so inadequate. But that's all I had.

Talking is painful. Explanations about my state of mind were dreary. I honestly didn't know what was wrong with me.

My horror went so much deeper than having breast cancer and being torn apart by the chemo. Like I write in the poem *Passing*, spoken by the character Levy in my movie, "I am empty, to the core like a dry vessel, cracked, broken" . . . and he ends it saying . . . Passing through existence no more."

At this point in time I didn't realize that God took everything away from me as promised from my 1987 Harmonic Conversion dream. I absolutely possessed no inner resources to save myself. The agony of Job's plight Job 5:22 *verse 4*:

For the arrows of the Almighty are within me
The poison whereof my spirit drinketh up
The terrors of God do set themselves in array against me.

And verse 13
Is it that I have no help in me?
And that sound wisdom is driven quite from me?

My hearing was scheduled. I prepared for my release. My weary brain thrashed around, pulling any remnants of intelligence that had managed to survive inside me. A plan. "What will I do when they let me out? How will I continue living?"

Work at Yogurtland. I like frozen yogurt. Work at Macy's. I shop there and I like the clothes. Work at Panera. I like bread. The thought of fresh bread surrounding me seemed comforting. Work as a therapist? Never.

CHAPTER 18
The End Is Near

Passing, the Movie

INTERIOR – BATHROOM –LATE AFTERNOON

CLEO is bending over the toilet throwing up. She has a kerchief covering her hairless head. She rises and heads for the Master closet inside the bedroom. She stops and observes her reflection in the mirror, shakes her head, and enters the closet. She closes the sliding door then lies on the floor in a fetal position.

EXTERIOR –OUTSIDE LEVY'S HOUSE -NIGHTTIME

LEVY sits in the passenger seat next to BRIAN in BRIAN'S car.

BRIAN
Do it now.

LEVY
(Stares straight ahead tapping a pencil on the window.)

BRIAN
(Grabs LEVY'S head and pushes him down to his crotch.)
NOW!

LEVY
(Unzips BRIAN'S fly. Takes his pencil and jabs BRIAN in the penis. BRIAN screams. LEVY pushes against BRIAN'S legs and stabs him again with the pencil. He quickly puts his hands on the car door and throws it open. Runs into the night.)

INTERIOR –OFFICE-NIGHTTIME

BILL
Bad news.

RORY
Looks up from the computer.

BILL
They couldn't raise the funds. No deal.

RORY
His head falls to his chest.
Okay. Thanks.

He gets up from the chair. Closes the computer. Walks to the door. Turns the light off. Closes the door.

Intelligence can't win all battles.

Without Hope
The Memoir

Three emotionless faces stared at me as we sat around the conference table. My heart was pounding. Conflicting thoughts whirled like a hurricane inside my head, but my demeanor needed to give the impression I was a calm, confident person. Being locked up, being watched 24 hours, being under the scrutiny of others was simply unbearable.

"Why did you want to hurt yourself, Sheryl?"

"I got cancer. Then the chemotherapy sent me into a state of severe depression. I couldn't sleep. I couldn't think." I rambled.

They nodded their heads, took their notes, and inevitably asked the critical question, "Do you still want to hurt yourself?"

"No. My family needs me. I have a plan. I know what I'll do when I'm released." All rehearsed lines.

"We'll let you know our decision in a few days."
Dismissed. A few days later, denied.

Back to the drudge of inpatient living: Wake up at 6 a.m. Blood pressure taken. Dress. Breakfast. Group therapy. Free time. Play games. Watch television. Lunch. Another group. Art therapy (hated it). Free time. Sometimes I played basketball outside. Sanity. My roommate and I were good players as we both had played in high school and college. Read books. Sanity. I lost myself in other peoples' stories.

I was told to attend AA meetings because it was determined I had a possible addiction to sleeping pills. Without the pills I couldn't sleep; a result of chemotherapy, nothing else. Never had a problem before. One day in group therapy, a young man talked about his addiction to heroin. As he described the supreme pleasure of floating on a high from the drug, I imagined drifting away on a cloud, being free of the psychic pain that tortured me. Heavenly.

As promised, I was released in two weeks. My hospital bill was $10,000. Before I left, I met with a therapist who found me an outpatient treatment center near my boyfriend. I had to go every day from 9 a.m. until 3 pm. I Agreed.

I packed up my meager belongings and waited. Finally freedom. I sat by the door all day waiting for my boyfriend to pick me up.

Evening settled in. I looked out from the thick pane glass, heared the buzz ring again and again as people came and went. Finally he emerged. I stood up quickly and wiped away my tears. As the door closed shut behind me, I felt a moment of happiness. The night air hit my face. Street noises chirped with normalcy.

Nothing was normal. My feet walked. My lips moved with words. I sat in the passenger side of the car, still a prisoner of to one thought. "I want to kill myself."

CHAPTER 19
Dead End

Passing, the Movie

INTERIOR – FAMILY ROOM – NIGHTTIME

CLEO lies limp on the couch in the family room watching television. Her two children sit on the rug below her, doing their homework. DANIEL walks in quickly with a briefcase. He looks at CLEO lying on the couch.

DANIEL
Why don't you lie down upstairs when you feel so bad?

CLEO
I want to be near the children.

RUTH
I got mommy a drink of water but she didn't drink it.

NOAH
I made her a peanut butter sandwich but she hasn't eaten it.

DANIEL
(He bends over her to whisper . . .)
The kids shouldn't see you like this. It upsets them. Let me call someone to take care of the situation.

CLEO
I'm only like this for a few days.

DANIEL
Go upstairs Cleo. Don't want to argue here. I'm calling someone to come over.

CLEO
(She doesn't move.)
I want to be at the heart of my family.

DANIEL
Have to go. I'm late for a patient.

RUTH
Bye Daddy

NOAH
We'll take care of Mommy.
DANIEL hurries out.

CLEO
NOAH, RUTH, come here.
(The two children stand up and CLEO puts her arms around them for a hug. She attempts to stand up).

CLEO
Let me get you something to eat. How about Mac and cheese?

RUTH
I'll eat the peanut butter sandwich.

NOAH
We'll share it.

CLEO
(She lies back down on the couch and closes her eyes.)

A DREAM SEQUENCE
CLEO is sitting in a room leaning back in a chair and all objects in the room begin to fly up and away as she desperately tries to hold onto everything. The room is empty but a Bible flies into her hands. A voice says, "Everything shall be taken away from you but never this."

BACK TO THE FAMILY ROOM

(CLEO opens her eyes and both children are standing over her).

NOAH
Mom, you were crying.

RUTH
Mommy!
(She falls into her mother's arms. NOAH follows.)

I had no answers, except one.

Dead End
The Memoir

I stood in a long line, waiting to talk with the psychiatrist at the West Covina outpatient facility. As I scanned the romm, my stomach was unsteady with anxiety. The people looked zoned out, desperate, drugged. I had to first speak with the psychiatrist to receive meds, then attend classes and group sessions all day long. The line inched slowly along. Like zombies, everyone stared straight ahead, creating an unapproachable, private space.

"Next," a male voice called to me.

The bald spot on the top of his head stared up at me as he leaned over my file.

"Are you still thinking about hurting yourself?"

"No."

His head jerked up. "Good. How are you sleeping?"

"Not good. I need a refill on Ambien."

"You got it. I'm going to refill your Atavan and Welbutrin."
I started counting pills.

"Do you need anything else? What are you taking for the follow up with your breast cancer?"

"Nothing."

"No tomoxifen?"

"No."

"Hmm. Why not?"

"Don't want the side effects."

"I'm giving you a prescription for it anyway. Anything else?"

"No."

"I am also going to have you take Klonopin to help with the anxiety."

Atavan and Klonopin, "Why not?" I thought. Just more pills to swallow.

"You need to come back next week."

"Sure."

"Good."

I headed to my first class. Entering the room, I felt awkward. I was the new kid on the block and all eyes were on me. There were only 12 people, so nowhere to hide. When it was my turn to talk, I told my story by rote memorization. I had cancer and chemo, I got depressed, left my marriage; couldn't work, had no purpose. The words tumble out with no emotion.

I was doomed. I saw nothing ahead of me, my past meant nothing. I used to head up these groups. I taught these classes. I knew the psychological principles I was being fed, but had no power to act on any of those principles.

I needed to collect the pills from the expanse of meds, wait two weeks so I had enough. I had a plan. My sister is the musical director for the theater performance at the high school where she teaches in Long Beach. I will tell my boyfriend that I am going to see the musical, then head to a quiet street in the neighborhood, and swallow every one of my pills.

But this time . . . I'll write a note.

CHAPTER 20
Entreaty

Passing, the Movie

EXTERIOR – CITY STREETS – NIGHT

LEVY runs wildly down the street looking over his shoulder. He turns the corner and finds a safe place to rest. He grabs his cell phone from his pocket and calls his mother's number. He gets a voicemail message. From his pocket, he takes out his notebook and his pencil. He looks up at the sky then begins to write furiously. He looks at his watch, looks up at the sky again as if he hears someone talking. He flips the notebook closed and stuffs it back in his pocket. He looks over his shoulder one more time then runs down the street.

INTERIOR – HARDWARE STORE – NIGHT

RORY walks through the hardware store briskly. He grabs some rope and throws it into his cart. He walks over to the ladders and grabs a tall ladder. He goes to the checkout counter and pays for his items. He rolls the cart out to the car. When he grasps the rope in his hands, he lifts it up to the heavens and shakes it toward the sky. Then he throws it into the trunk with the ladder and slams the hood down. He gets into the car and drives away.

INTERIOR –BEDROOM –NIGHT

CLEO lies in her bed looking up at the ceiling. Her arms are folded over her chest and she is rubbing the catheter that has been placed in her chest for the chemo. She puts her hands together in prayer and moans softly.

Like all the characters of *Passing*,
I believe the end is near.

Entreaty
The Memoir

The night arrived. I walked calmly into the kitchen and opened the drawer that contained the Ziplock bags. Carefully I pulled out three of those bags and entered the bathroom, closing the door behind me. I opened the cabinet drawer where the pill bottles were stored. I popped open each lid then poured pills into one plastic at a time. When all the bag were filled, I hid them in my purse and walked out of the bathroom. My unsuspecting boyfriend sat at his computer in the den, typing away.

"I'm going to my sister's performance now," I said.

"Have fun."

I drove the car to a gas station and bought two bottles of water. I thought about which neighborhood I should park my car. I drove through the streets, looking at the houses, taking inventory of how many people walked on the sidewalk. I finally decided where to park my car. I sat still. I took out a piece of paper and scribble a note to my boyfriend and children.

All I could do is apologize, thank my ex-husband for being a good father, thank my boyfriend for caring about me, tell my children I loved them.

I swallowed pills, drank water, swallowed more pills, gagged, swallowed pills. Didn't stop. Didn't think. It was time to leave behind the gaping hole that became my soul. No more pills. My brain was fuzzy. I reclined back in my seat and I said goodbye. I closed my eyes and surrendered to death.

"Why didn't you let her die?" Satan looks up at God imploringly.

God smiles. "I promised him she wouldn't die this time"

"Why didn't you let her die?" Satan repeats.

"Someone was waiting for her, someone who has been waiting for his love . . . for centuries."

"Who?"

God smiles.
"Someone who loves me and is not your friend."

CHAPTER 21
Memory's Meeting

Passing, the Movie

EXTERIOR – WOODS –JUST BEFORE DAWN

RORY walks into the grove of trees with the ladder and rope. HE looks around for the appropriate tree to place the ladder. As RORY walks over to the tree, he stops suddenly. A woman lies on the ground. A bottle of tequila and an empty pill bottle lay next to her. He bends over her. Her chest moves up and down slightly. He closes his eyes and clenches his fists, then walks by her. He sets up the ladder. LEVY runs through the trees in the distance. He sees RORY placing the ladder under the tree. LEVY stops. He watches RORY take the rope and tie it over a branch. He notices CLEO lying still on the ground. RORY climbs the ladder, pulls the rope over his neck. LEVY turns away and runs toward the river.

All stories converge
at the same place.

Memory's Meeting
The Memoir

My eyes opened. A person was sitting beside me. Tubes poked into my arm. A catheter jabbed my inners. A thin hospital gown cloaked my naked body. Alive. I am alive.

I turned my head toward the woman sitting in the chair. She smiled.

"I am watching you. Someone needs to be by your side until it's determined you're safe."

No privacy. A psych babysitter. She settled back into the chair.

Horror. I felt suffocated. I turned on the television. Time passed and this woman's shift ended, and another woman replaced her. A psychiatrist stopped by to check on me. My pee bag was emptied by nurses.

If hell existed on earth, I was living it.

I'm on watch for 72 hours. I counted the hours when the catheter could be taken out of me and I was able to walk to the bathroom by myself. I counted the hours when my psych babysitter would be taken away.

"Your car was towed," my boyfriend said.
I stare at him.

"A woman walking her dog found you. She saw you sleeping in the car and called the police. They had to break the window to open the door and get you out."

"Hmmm."

"I found the note you wrote. I took it."

I blinked my eyes.

"Your sister called asking if you were going to the show. I told her you had left. She said you never arrived. That's when I called the police. They told me where your car had been found, and that you were in the hospital."

I listened.

"I don't understand. I don't know what's wrong with you."

Neither did I.

"This time you're going to be locked up here, in a West Covina in-patient treatment center."

146

I didn't care.

One cell for another. My internal prison followed me everywhere. The month was May. The year was 2009. I had spent the last five months desperately attempting to free myself from the prison sentence of life. I am a Capricorn. One characteristic we are known for is tenacity. No matter, death was now my goal.

CHAPTER 22
The Curtain Rises

Passing, **the Movie**

EXTERIOR – THE WOODS – MORNING

RORY jumps off the ladder with the rope around his neck and hangs himself. A snapping sound echoes.

EXTERIOR – THE RIVER –MORNING

LEVY pulls the trigger . . . the gun blast cracks through the air . . . LEVY falls into the water.

EXTERIOR – THE WOODS –MORNING

CLEO is on her knees. Her body quivers and convulses as if she sees and hears both boys' death. She falls face down to the ground.

The end is sometimes the beginning.

The Curtain Rises
The Memoir

Mother's Day, 2009. Visiting hours. My eyes captured the three figures walking down the sidewalk outside the inpatient facility's cafeteria. The two children flanked my ex-husband on each side. They were holding hands. I rushed to the greeting room. I sat on a chair and waited. The trio walked in. My feet pressed against the floor but I couldn't stand. My son walked over and hugged me. My daughter watched cautiously by her father's side. I stood up and walked over to my daughter and hugged her. My ex looked on silently.

The children's faces lit up for a moment. Then my son reached into a bag and held out to me a huge chocolate bar.

"Can you eat this here, Ma?"

I nodded my head. Everyone smiled.

No memory of the conversation between us for the next hour.

I only remembered rushing back to the cafeteria, holding my Mother's Day candy bar and watching the children and my ex walk away the same way they came, each holding his hand. My heart was broken.

CHAPTER 23
A Way Back

Passing, the Movie

EXT. A SWIMMING POOL – EARLY MORNING

NOAH and RUTH are at the edge of the pool looking down anxiously. CLEO bursts through the water's surface coming up for air.

NOAH
MA! MA! What were you doing?

RUTH
Didn't know you could hold your breath that long.

CLEO is disoriented at first. She quickly turns her head from side to side as if looking for someone. When she sees her children she relaxes and sighs.

CLEO
Don't worry kids. It's a game I play. See how long I can survive under water.

NOAH
HATE THAT GAME, MA! DON'T DO THAT AGAIN.

RUTH
Are you okay? Did you die?

CLEO
(Steps out of pool and hugs both children.)

No, love . . . I didn't die. I feel as if, (she pauses and thinks) . . . I passed myself by, as if I'm brand new.

RUTH
We have a new Mommy.

NOAH
(Under his breath)
New . . . Maman est renaissant.

CLEO
Who wants breakfast?
The two children nod yes. They walk away. Pool water shimmers in the sunlight.

Just like Cleo, who
emerged from death's hold,
I, too, found a way back.

A Way Back
The Memoir

Dying. It's not going to happen. Even though I lived through this third attempt, I still contemplated death on a daily basis. I sat in a parking lot near my boyfriend's house then got out of the car, climbed to the top of the roof and imagined jumping. When I drove on an overpass, I thought about driving off. I'd go to the end of a dock and want to throw myself into the water. And unexpectedly, white feathers would continue to appear. It was a sign from above that someone was watching over me.

"I guess I'm not going to die, but I have no idea how I'm going to live."

***

Four years had passed. I forced myself to go to my children's open houses at school, my daughter's water polo games, and both children's high school graduations. I barely talked. I gained weight from lack of exercise. I dressed in dull colors and looked disheveled. The tension between my boyfriend and me escalated, and eventually became unbearable for me. I had no answers to his repeated question, "What are you going to do with your life?" I mainly stayed at my condo in Laguna Woods. I hated the pressure. For 24 hours the television blasted non-stop. I'd gaze at the screen; I'd fall asleep; I'd order takeout; I'd read; I'd watch more television.

One morning in February 2013, I was lying on the couch, and through my front door, in came my boyfriend holding five garbage bags. He threw the bags on the living room floor. "I've packed up all your belongings. I'm done. I can't take it anymore. We're through."

All my fears took over. "No one will ever want me again. I will have to endure this miserable existence for the rest of my life." But this was my first step back to my life. Little did I know God was slowly but surely returning my soul. I was being reborn.

CHAPTER 24
Rebirth

Passing, the Movie

INTERIOR – BOOKSTORE – DAY

SHERYL ARONSON, AUTHOR/PSYCHOTHERAPIST stands at the podium. She looks out to the audience.

SHERYL
The portal to the grave opens…
(She pauses. She stares straight ahead.)

SHERYL
I walk inside, completely unaware of my dissent into the hades of my existence.
(A pause)

SHERYL
Yet, even though I walked through hell, soulless, with no hope of ever feeling a grain of happiness, a miracle occurs in the year 2013. When I look back, I have no explanation except this is God's grace. God had taken away everything from me as my 1987 dream prophesied; but now, I was being given my life back slowly, over time. I took infinitesimal baby steps, discovering what made my inner being feel alive, passionate. I didn't seek therapy. I didn't take drugs to alter my mood. It's as if a parent's hand keeps gently pushing me forward, yet at the same time allowing me to move at my own pace. Listen, if I had come to me as a patient after I had tried to take my life three times, had been hospitalized, had gone through breast cancer, divorce, severe isolation, depression, anxiety, I would tell this client that she needs to see me at least three times a week for a few months; put her on anti-depressants, have her see a psychiatrist, and tell her to attend as many support groups as possible, fearing for her sanity. I wouldn't even begin to guess when she would feel healed—maybe not in this lifetime!

Here's what was so strange. I wasn't praying or making requests to God about what I wanted or needed; because I hadn't known for so long what I did want or even need; and any conscious thoughts I may have had were buried away in a subterranean grave. But the universe kept dropping gifts — materially, emotionally, spiritually into my lap . . . which mystified me.

SATAN TURNS TO GOD

SATAN
You. You. YOU! YOU!

GOD
Always here.

SATAN
Deceived me.

GOD
No. I kept my promise.

SATAN
TO WHOM?

GOD
To you. To Sheryl.

SATAN
Her soul belonged to me.

GOD
Through you, man loses his sight, his heart, his love, and his soul, yet I am always here. I will always allow man to be reborn, eternally inside every precious moment of his existence. Sheryl went down to the grave . . . naked . . . alone . . . yet she passed through the canal of darkness and now stands on the stage of her life, exposed, raw, and ready for a new turn.

SATAN
Hmmph! (SATAN looks around and spies another person down below on earth. He points wildly.) Take everything away from him. See if he still believes in you!

GOD
(Smiles) And so it begins.

EXT. – BOOKSTORE – DAY

SHERYL reaches down and puts a Bible on the podium.

SHERYL
The Rabbi gave me this Bible when we spoke about THE BOOK OF JOB. That was back in the spring of 2008 when my life was unraveling. I wrote about that moment in my memoir. I had never opened this Bible; I had never read it or looked inside it. However, I have carried this Bible with me from place to place . . .

And it has sat on my bookshelf above my bed. Until May 2014.

(SHERYL pauses and looks intently at the audience.)

The universe exists in parallel realities. Each one influences the other.

Rebirth
The Memoir

My boyfriend walked out the door. I picked up the cell phone and called my sister.

"What's wrong?" she asked nervously as soon as she heard my voice.

"Done. We're done. He dropped off garbage bags with all my clothes. Dumped them on my living room floor. I Don't know what to do," Forcing the words out through a haze of tears.

"Pack a suitcase and you'll stay in a hotel near me for a week. Let me find you a place." She hung up and called back in half an hour. "Okay. You'll be a few exits from my house. I'll see you every day after I get back from school. You'll be fine. I want to make sure you're safe."

"I'm not going to hurt myself."

Silence. "Just get yourself over here. You're going to be okay."

My body sunk deep into the soft cushions of the couch. Each muscle was filled with dread and I felt like I was sinking in quicksand. Pack a suitcase? I barely dressed now. What was I going to bring? My feet dragged as I made my way to the closet. Black. I chose whatever pants and shirts went with black. More important than clothes were books. Reading equals pleasure. I grabbed ten novels from the bookcase that was over my bed and tossed them on top of my clothes.

As I drove to North Hollywood, I thought about nothing. The freeway was one long stretch of an infinite road leading nowhere. There was some comfort though. My sister was waiting for me at the other end. She stood outside her house when I pulled up. She hugged me then looked into my eyes with concern.

"You won't hurt yourself while you're staying out here? Promise me."

"I promise, sis."

"Okay, follow me and we'll drive to the motel. You'll have a television, bathroom, and a place to cook. I'll be close by. We can go to the movies. We can eat dinner together." She handed me a care package full of food, drinks, laundry detergent . . . everything I needed for a week's stay.

For a few minutes, I felt safe. For a few minutes, I felt as if I might not want to die. For a few minutes, I felt a tiny hint of relief.

After my sister left, and I was all alone in my cozy motel room, my heart began to pound, my head started to throb, and I fell on the bed.

Books. Where are my books? My reading marathon began. I went nowhere unless my sister drove me. I stayed inside everyday, reading and watching television until my sister knocked on the door and we went out. When we returned from the movies one afternoon, I saw a rod in front of my eyes, a brown, dangling branch-like rod. I blinked. The image remained.

"I can't get rid of this image." I told my sister in a panic.

We rushed to the emergency room. Six hours later, the figure blinked on and off, and I felt so much anxiety. My heart felt crushed. Would I have to live with these dangling rods forever in my mind's eye?

The week came to an end, and it was time to go home. Where was my home? I packed my suitcase, took the extra food I hadn't eaten, and drove back to Laguna Woods, Orange County. The disturbing eye projections had diminished somewhat. I decided to do something I hadn't done in five years. I called a friend. I had only allowed three of my local friends to interact with me since 2009. No one knew where I was or what had happened to me. I dropped out. Being on the computer turned my stomach. I had no idea how to operate this device.

Truly, I didn't want to exist.

When I opened the door to my living room, the five garbage bags looked like green blobs. I maneuvered around them. Soon I was back on my couch, the television purred, and I picked up a book. Then I remembered, call my girlfriend. I dialed her number.

"Hello," a familiar voice answered.

"Hello. This is Sheryl. Can we get together?"

"My God, Sheryl! I can't believe this. It's been years. Where are you? How have you been? Are you okay?"

"I haven't been well. I would like to see you. Start going out again."

"Yes. Let's do that. Come over whenever you'd like."

"How about next week?"

"Absolutely."

When I put the phone down, I was both nervous and excited. What will I say? How do I explain my dilemma? I continued reading until the morning. I slept only a few hours a day. The chemo had totally ruined my system and I needed heavy-duty sleeping pills to get just five hours of sleep. I stayed on my couch all day reading books. I went to the library, checked out 15 more books, and by the end of the week I had read them all. I started with the A's then worked my way down the alphabet. The couch became my domain. I hid away in the safe cocoon of my house.

Finally, the day arrived to see my friend. I felt unattractive. She hugged me as soon as I walked through the door.

"We're going to a St. Patrick's Day party," she informed me.
I was petrified. I had to interact with people, which at the time was still extremely difficult for me. I only wore black pants because that's the only thing that fit, and a long, baggy, green shirt. When we entered the party, I notice there were mostly couples. But there was one man who seemed to be by himself. He sat with us during dinner. And for some strange reason, he turned his attention to me.

I was confused. I looked terrible. I barely spoke. My friend seemed to be the one who was talking to him. But he kept asking me questions, including me in the conversation. I had no idea how he could be attracted to me. I was practically mute.

To my surprise, he asked me for my number. I gave it to him. I figured it was a good sign that a man was still attracted to me, even though I thought I looked depressed.

After a few months had passed, I decided to join a book club. I was terrified to speak in front of people, even though I used to lead seminars as a psychotherapist. For the first time in seven years I thought about what actually interested me. I was resurfacing from a dark, empty place.

Dates were painful with my new friend. He wanted me to talk and I couldn't. I still felt stifled. I was like Rip Van Winkle waking up after so many years asleep. I forced myself to date him, forcing out of me only a few words.

"Why don't you talk?" he demanded impatiently. "Why don't you show me some affection?" This was another one of his complaints.

He threatened to end the relationship many times but we kept dating. I felt like I was slowly waking up out of a coma. I noticed that my life had been handed back to me. God was gently reminding me who I was, and I suddenly got a glimpse of the future. It was too early to feel happy or to trust that these positive emotions would last. However, I gave thanks to God for relieving me of the heavy burden and anxiety that had been weighing me down for so many years.

August 2013 – For the first time since 2003, I was able to get on a plane by myself. I had been paranoid about going anywhere alone when I left my marriage up until this moment. I just never felt safe or secure enough. Making the decision to see my son in Boston and return to the city where I lived as a college student and young adult was huge.

The first night I arrived in the city, I walk to the Boston Commons. My heart was filled with joy. I remembered how I used to hike around this town for hours when I was a college student and it felt like that free-spirited college girl had returned. I observed a lone sax player. He was standing on the bridge, overlooking the pond and blowing some jazz. I smiled. It felt like I had come home.

In fact, the next day I invited a man I had spoken to briefly in the elevator at the hotel where I was staying to join me for breakfast. I didn't have the confidence to do this the last six months after my boyfriend dumped me. The gentleman turned out to be a sports writer from Amsterdam, covering the Boston Red Sox for his newspaper. I couldn't believe my fate. I loved baseball my entire life, and had played softball, too. Our meeting opened the door for me to recapture my love of sports and my love for writing. I realized that I could attract a man that I was attracted to. Hans said to me, "I've never met any woman who knows as much about baseball as you do." We started corresponding after he returned to Holland, and through our emails, I began to start writing again. Meeting Hans helped to break off my relationship with the gentleman I had met at the party. I started talking again at parties and social gatherings, and I even flirted a bit. My trip to Boston was a turning point. I decided to take a writing class. I joined the men's softball practice by my home. I even went online to try my luck at dating again. I visited Hans in Europe the following summer. I began exercising again and was losing weight.

October 2013
The Thursday before Halloween, I walked down the hill from the Ritz-Carlton. As I was taking my daily two-hour walk to the beach, a young man dressed in black walked beside me and struck up a conversation. I talked with him and realized he was flirting with me. I could have been his mother, but I certainly enjoyed the idea that this was happening. The flirting turned into a mini date that very afternoon. He was interested in me, and I discovered he was in the film industry. From our meeting, we had a torrid love affair. He asked me to write two short movie scripts that I had

that I developed and we produced together. My girlfriend who owns her own publishing company asked me what would be my dream if I had one. I said to be a writer. She announced, "I'm taking you on to write articles for my websites as an intern." I now write daily with plenty of assignments.

In June, I could barely talk. In the fall, my self-confidence came back and a seed was planted. It's as if time sped up, causing me to emerge strong, secure, and whole again. The process mystified me; yet I am profoundly grateful because peace and happiness has offered my inner self a permanent residence.

Nov – Dec 2013
I started writing the movies: *Passing & Down to the Grave*. A good candidate for a relationship appeared on Match.com. He lived in Washington, DC. As I turned sixty, I felt sexy and beautiful. My enthusiasm for life continued, and every time looked in the mirror, I liked what I saw. On December 28th, I celebrated my birthday with 13 of my friends whom I had shut out of my life for seven years. Ten years had passed since my 50th birthday when my life began to unravel.

I'd been communicating with Hans almost daily via emails. I was still involved romantically with the young filmmaker. I looked like a completely different person. No longer that disheveled, depressed, suicidal woman who took refuge on her couch just eleven months before. God had handed me my life back.

Jan 2014
The pre-production of Passing & Down to the Grave was underway. I was flirting, communicating with the man from Washington, D.C., on a daily basis and we were forming a relationship. I finalized my plans to visit with Hans in August. I felt happy for no reason other than just being happy.

I began writing the introduction to my memoir *Passing Myself Down to the Grave*.

Feb 2014

Valentine's Day weekend, the man from Washington D.C., came to visit. A disaster. He wasn't the open, flirtatious, warm person he seemed to be over the phone. Instead he was a distant, critical, non-appreciative male who acted like he wanted nothing to do with me from the moment he got off the plane. The young man with I was co-producing the movies with turned on me. He criticized me in front of the actors. According to him, I couldn't do anything right; in spite of the fact that I organized the entire production from casting to feeding the actors on set to writing the scripts. The tension between us kept building until it finally erupted.

We were filming *Down to the Grave* the weekend after Valentine's Day. We finished filming in LA, but by this time he was barely speaking to me. He headed up to San Francisco to film his friend's movie and expected me to find a location for the movie *Passing*. We needed a tree that someone could tie a noose and do a mock hanging. We also needed a body of water and a forest setting in either LA or Orange County. Neither existed unless I paid large sums of money for permits to be able to legally film in a state park.

The man from D.C. dumped me, saying the weekend didn't turn out well. No kidding. Despite these very disturbing setbacks, I remained positive and hopeful. An emotional resiliency had been established inside of me. Before, these issues would have had disastrous consequences.

The next day I was contacted by Morocco from North Carolina who turned into a six month, serious relationship.

The young filmmaker returned from San Francisco to begin filming *Passing* in the last weekend in February. The production was never completed because he walked away without a word after deciding a location I had found for the last scene of the day was inadequate. He called a few days later, telling me to give up my producer and my writing credits so that he could be named sole creator of both movies. I hung up on him. No movies. I never saw any of the footage, and all the money I had invested in the movie was lost. But all was not lost . . .

March 2013
I returned to Boston. I visited my son at Tufts. I went to Harvard to see Herbie Hancock, who was lecturing as a Poet Laureate, and I had ambitions of writing an article on him once again. (In 1980, I had written a cover story on Mr. Hancock for a magazine called *Modern Recording*.) Plus, I arranged to interview Garrison Fewell, an old boyfriend who was a guitarist/composer/ professor at Berklee School of Music, and author of the book *Outside Music, Inside Voices.*

As fate would have it, I reunited with Terri-Lyne Carrington, (a three-time Grammy winner, jazz drummer, composer, and producer). Terri-Lyne was the subject of my very first professional article back in the late 70s. She was only thirteen years old and already a professional musician when I conducted that interview with her. To my supreme surprise and pleasure, Terri-Lyne was scheduled to play with Herbie Hancock on the last night of his lecture at Harvard. After the show, I sought out her father Sonny Carrington. I hadn't seen him since 1979. I found him, tapped him on his shoulder and said, "Sonny, do you remember me?"

He laughed, "Why Sheryl, I always wondered what happened to you after you moved to Los Angeles."

I asked him, "Can I write another article on your daughter?"

We both laughed. Thirty-five years had passed but Terri-Lyne still remembered me and agreed to the interview. Since that time, I became a journalist and had written several articles; and she won another Grammy in 2015 for producing Diane Reeves' CD, *Beautiful Life.*

I spent one week in Boston, during which time I was able interview Garrison Fewell in a television studio just outside of Boston. I also created an opportunity for myself on a sports television program, that was being filmed a few doors down. Before I left California, I researched the television station and discovered they had a sports program that focused on baseball. I wrote a poem called *Fenway Park for Hans*, who was a huge fan of the Red Sox. I decided to take my poem with me and see if there was any interest. One of the sportscasters was there, waiting to go into the studio. I introduced myself and recited my poem to him. He loved it. He invited me on the show after I interviewed Garrison. I had to studio hop, but I made both situations happen.

The funny thing was: I'M A YANKEES FAN, so I had to talk about the Yankees with the Red Sox sportscasters. After my week in Boston, I visited Morocco in Raleigh, North Carolina, for one week. We seemed to get along well, and a relationship evolved. I felt like I was on top of life again.

May 2014

Morocco visited me in California for three weeks. While he was here, we had a disagreement, which forced me to go into my room to meditate. While I was sitting on my bed, I heard a voice, "Go get the Bible the Rabbi gave you and read it." So I grabbed the bible from the shelf above me and noticed some business cards acting as book marks inside. I opened it to that page. It was THE BOOK OF JOB. My heart raced. Why had I been told to read this now?

Job was lamenting to God about how his life wasn't worth living without God's presence. Wow. This is exactly how I felt during my 12 years of despair, before and after my bout with breast cancer. At the bottom of the last page the most miraculous thing happened. There was this Bible passage:

The eye of him that seeth me shall behold me no more,
while thine eyes are upon me, I am gone (this is exactly how I
felt for 12 years). As the cloud is consumed and vanisheth away,
so he that (goeth down to the grave) . . . shall come up no more.
(BOOK OF JOB, 7:10, v.8 –v.9)

DOWN TO THE GRAVE WAS THE TITLE OF THE MOVIE I HAD WRITTEN THAT WAS NEVER MADE.

My eyes welled up with tears. I couldn't believe what I had just read. Suddenly the horrible experiences that had terrorized me for twelve years, and had caused me to attempt suicide repeatedly had new meaning. The workings of God's hands fell upon me. I felt blessed. I felt God's miracles envelop my entire being.

When I wrote the two short films, *Passing* and *Down to the Grave*, I had shocked myself with the subjects I had chosen. I was always a romantic, a happily ever after girl, but these two movies explored death, murder, and suicide. I didn't question the stories when they popped into my mind, because at this point I believed ideas had been sent to me through divine inspiration.

In the movie, *Down to the Grave*, when I wrote those lines coming out of Hector's mouth as he explains his philosophy of killing to his best friend Joshua, I shocked myself. Why did I write this? Now I know why. Here are the lines: "The weak, they go down to the grave, but we're strong so we're going to killer's heaven."

From then on, I decided to focus diligently on my memoir. The the title appeared when I prayed about the book: *Passing Myself Down to the Grave* combines the titles of both my movies.

My life for the past three years had been full of miracles. I am now a staff writer for *The Hollywood 360* and have my own entertainment blog called "Arting Around" in *Agenda* magazine. I am finally living my fifth grade dream as a professional writer. I have travelled the world, interviewing musicians, actors, directors, writers, fine artists, etc., writing articles for *The Hollywood 360*, and becoming friends with so many wonderfully creative people. I am living the life I had envisioned when I was in my twenties and first moved to Los Angeles with the goal of becoming a professional writer, working in the music and entertainment industry.

My spirit is soaring again, wiser and aware of depression's depths. *Passing Myself Down to the Grave* is my story.

P.S. The relationship with Morocco didn't work out.

P.P.S. I did visit Hans in Amsterdam in August 2014. By that time he and I were just friends.

Passing, the Movie

EXT. BOOKSTORE – DAY

SHERYL ARONSON
She holds the Bible in her hands and opens it up.

SHERYL
I want to read you a passage from this Bible. I opened it up to this very page. I heard God's voice tell me to take the Holy Scriptures down from the bookshelf after I had just argued with my boyfriend in May 2014. A business card was stuck in the book so I decided this was what I needed to read. (Book of Job, 7:10, v.4-v.10)

When I lie down, I say: When shall I arise?
But the night is long, and I am full of tossings to and fro unto the dawning of the day,
My flesh is clothed with worms and clods of dust;
My skin closest up and breaketh out afresh.
My days are swifter than a weaver's shuttle,
And are spent without hope.
Oh remember that my life is a breath;
Mine eye shall no more see good.
The eye of him that seeth me shall behold me no more'
While thine eyes are upon me, I am gone.
As the cloud is consumed and vanisheth away,

(SHERYL STOPS AND LOOKS AT THE AUDIENCE.)

SO HE…THAT GOETH DOWN TO THE GRAVE…

(THE AUDIENCE GASPS.)

SHALL COME UP NO MORE
He shall return no more to his house,
Neither shall his place know him anymore.
This is exactly how I felt about my life. But I did rise. I was reborn. As God gave Job's life back to him, my life was given back to me. I ended up PASSING MYSELF DOWN TO THE GRAVE.

EXT – BOOKSTORE – DAY
In the audience CLEO sits with her family. RORY sits with a new girlfriend by his side. LEVY sits with his mother.

The End.

CHAPTER 25

Afterword

January 2016

Miracles continue to bless my life in abundance. I want to share a story. On the afternoon I finished writing in my memoir about my experiences with chemotherapy, I decided to have lunch at the Zinc Café in Laguna Beach. I felt exhausted and emotionally drained as I relived the ghastly experience that chemo had put me through. Next to my table on the patio sat two men with whom I we struck up a conversation. We spoke about traveling to Paris and the fun times we had there on our individual journeys.

After a while, I asked them what they did for a living. The first gentleman said he had an unusual gift shop in Orange. I turn to the other gentleman and he answered, "I'm an oncologist." I found this highly unusual, but knew immediately that God had a hand in this meeting. I told the doctor about my horrible experiences with chemotherapy, and he said that if I had been diagnosed today, chemo wouldn't have been required for my early stage of breast cancer. Interesting. I asked him where his practice was located. He replied, "Irvine."

Again, highly unusual because that's exactly where my oncologist's practice was located. So I asked him, "Perhaps you know Dr. Teteff?"

He smiled and answered, "I'm in practice with her."

I could not believe what I was hearing. I told them how I had described the oncologist's waiting room in my memoir; and the doctor pointed to the other man and said, "He designed that waiting room so it would be soothing."

There were so many amazing stories that could have filled up another book.

Did I mention that God and Satan weren't entirely finished with me? I mistakenly thought everything that could be taken away from me had been. Well, I was wrong.

ABOUT THE AUTHOR

Sheryl Aronson, MFT is an award-winning, entertainment reporter for *The Hollywood 360* and *Agenda* magazine. She writes profiles on celebrities in the entertainment industry. Sheryl reviews concerts, film, theater, and covers red carpet entertainment events in Los Angeles. She has traveled extensively, reporting from the East Coast, Europe, and Africa.

Sheryl is an acclaimed, published poet and has published articles on many iconic jazz musicians, including Herbie Hancock and Maynard Ferguson in the magazine *Modern Recording*; and on Terri-Lyne Carrington, a jazz prodigy, in *Soul Teen* magazine and *Agenda* magazine. As a Marriage, Family Therapist, Sheryl Aronson has published articles on relationships and women's self-esteem for local publications in Orange County, including the *Orange County Metropolitan*, *Awareness* magazine, and *Beach Cities/Valley* magazine.

Sheryl Aronson has also been a Marriage Family Therapist for over 25 years. She has a private practice in Orange County and Los Angeles counties, specializing in relationships and women's self-esteem. She has created and led Relationship

Workshops, plus Women and Self-Esteem Workshops throughout Orange County, California. She was a featured guest and Relationship Expert on the *Montel Williams* show and *The Berman Sisters* television show in Los Angeles.

In Sheryl's own words when describing her private practice: "My practice focuses on building, healing, and developing strong personal and intimate relationships - which are truly the cornerstone of psychological, physical, and spiritual health. My specialty is working with couples and giving them the skills necessary to sustain a successful relationship.

Sheryl Aronson

I also have a strong interest in women's issues, especially in the development of improved SELF-ESTEEM throughout all of their transitions in life. While I am especially interested in helping women, I also have a bulk of experience in helping men through their relationship and professional difficulties. I offer unique interactive communication that promotes positive change.

I am very active in my approach toward helping each client find his or her own solution. I can quickly assess situations and find appropriate resolutions. I can help turn negative mindsets into positive and workable ones that will leave one ready to live a more satisfying life. No problem is unsolvable!"

Sheryl's Websites and Social Media:
sherylaronsonauthor.com
saronsonmft@yahoo.com
https://www.facebook.com/sheryl.aronson.444
https://www.instagram.com/sherylaronson/
http://thehollywood360.com/author/sheryl-aronson/
http://www.agendamag.com/blog-category/arting-around/
https://twitter.com/jazzinaround444

77791289R00112

Made in the USA
San Bernardino, CA
28 May 2018